PEACE AND CONFLICT:
JOURNAL OF PEACE PSYCHOLOGY

Volume 11, Number 3   2005

SPECIAL ISSUE
Peace Psychology in Germany
Klaus Boehnke, Daniel Fuss, & Angela Kindervater, *Guest Editors*

T0347212

Psychology Press
Taylor & Francis Group
New York London

PEACE AND CONFLICT: JOURNAL OF PEACE PSYCHOLOGY, *11*(3), 227

A Welcome Exposure to Peace Psychology in Germany

Richard V. Wagner
Bates College

One of the joys of editing *Peace and Conflict: Journal of Peace Psychology* comes from having the opportunity and the privilege of reading and learning about the wealth of research and ideas that we in North America are seldom exposed to. As a mid-20th century graduate student and young professional, I knew about the "Gestalt brothers", Piaget, Freud and Jung, and Horney, who, by the 1960s, seemed a part of psychology's ancient history. Slowly, research from France, the UK, even the USSR, appeared during the 1970s. International psychology burst on my mental scene, however, in the early 1980s via political psychology, followed shortly thereafter by the developing field of peace psychology.

We are indeed fortunate once again to be able to devote an issue of *Peace and Conflict: Journal of Peace Psychology* to a sampling of the efforts of peace psychologists in another national setting–in this case, Germany. In the introductory article of this issue, Klaus Boehnke, one of our review editors extraordinaire, and his colleagues, Daniel Fuss and Angela Kindervater, recount the development of peace psychology during and after the reunification of the two Germanys. The history is not unlike that experienced in the United States: initial alignment with political science, evolving interdisciplinarity, debates about the merits of promoting peace psychology as yet another subdivision of the general field of psychology, the politicization within that general field of the term "peace", publication of field-defining handbooks, and strong alliances with other peace psychology organizations world-wide.

Klaus Boehnke has gathered research articles from an excellent cross-section of German peace psychologists: established pioneers, creative and energetic newcomers, quantitative and qualitative analysts, and professionals whose careers evolved on each side of the former East-West national divide. We are indebted to Klaus Boehnke and his colleagues for their exceptional efforts in organizing this stimulating special issue, as well as to the numerous peace social scientists whose contributions illuminate a realm of peace research with which many of us are too little familiar.

"(T)he ... cost of our reluctance to theorize and go beyond the information given: our relatively modest voice in the general intellectual debate about societal issues. The nonspecialists do not care much about the elegance of our designs and the sophistication of our procedures. They want to know what it all means and whether our take-home message is novel and exciting."

Arie W. Kruglanski, "That 'vision thing': The state of theory in social and personality psychology at the edge of the new millennium." *Journal of Personality and Social Psychology*, 2001, p. 873.

PEACE AND CONFLICT: JOURNAL OF PEACE PSYCHOLOGY, *11*(3), 229–237

INTRODUCTION

Peace Psychology in Germany

Klaus Boehnke, Daniel Fuss, Angela Kindervater
International University Bremen

What readers hold in hand is a special issue of *Peace and Conflict: Journal of Peace Psychology*, devoted to Peace Psychology in Germany. By giving it this obvious title, we imply that the issue exclusively reports research conducted in Germany, in the sense that scholars working at institutions in Germany have been solicited to contribute. This excludes neither non-German nationals nor research with non-German subjects but it implies that the issue encompasses contributions from scientists working or having worked in a German institutional framework.

Although this may not seem too obvious in a journal devoted to peace psychology, the mere fact that the special issue uses the denotational term *peace psychology* in its title does need a brief explanation. Some 13 years ago, the first guest editor argued that psychological studies related to the war and peace topic should be categorized as *psychological peace research*, rather than as *peace psychology* (Boehnke, 1992). This plea, issued at the beginning of the 1990s, built on two basic arguments.

On the one hand, the usage of the term *psychological peace research* implied an acknowledgment of the fact that phenomena like war and peace are (inter)societal phenomena, not consequences of intrapsychic processes (Eberwein & Reichel, 1976). Just as there will hardly be anything like "peace biology" dealing with remedies against aggression genes that may cause human warfare, it seems plausible not to deal with psychological dimensions of war and peace exclusively within the framework of a scientific subdomain of psychology. Peace is not a matter of psychologically controlling aggressive drives, nor are wars a consequence of neurotic leaders being unable to restrain their innate aggressive tendencies or to resolve

Correspondence should be sent to Klaus Boehnke, Professor of Social Science Methodology, School of Humanities and Social Sciences, International University Bremen, Campus Ring 1, D–28759 Bremen, Germany. E-mail: K.Boehnke@iu-bremen.de

conflicts with other leaders in a rational way. The choice of the denotation *psychological peace research* was meant to convey that the leadership of political science is, and has to be, accepted when psychologists deal with problems of war and peace. It suggested at the same time that psychology has to take an interdisciplinary approach when dealing with the peace topic. This argument still holds some 13 years later.

On the other hand, the then-choice of *psychological peace research* instead of *peace psychology* to denote the academic discipline at stake, also reflected the peculiarities of a specific historic situation. The Cold War era had ended just months before the publication date of the 1992 article, when the Soviet Union was dissolved in December 1991. There was still a ready knowledge of Cold War rhetoric. Between the early 1950s and 1990, *peace* was often used as an agitation and propaganda term by the East, the so-called "real socialist" bloc, when describing its basic political orientation. The West combated this by using *freedom* as a term with a similar function. In subterranean connotations, the juxtaposition of the two terms meant that the East would sacrifice freedom for the sake of peace and the West—if need be—would sacrifice peace for freedom. In the East, this meant that everybody who argued for freedom was declared an agent of capitalism (to say the least), and in the West anybody arguing for peace was in the danger of being labeled a communist. In this situation, which was still quite fresh in the early 1990s, it seemed safer not to label one's scientific area of interest "peace psychology" but rather "psychological peace research," because peace research as a part of political science had more credibility in the social sciences than one could assume a newcomer like peace psychology would have. The reluctance to jump forward and claim the existence of, or indeed issue a demand for the foundation of, a new discipline of applied psychology—namely peace psychology—could, at that time, have been counterproductive.

Meanwhile, times have changed, not only in Germany but in most scientific communities. Boehnke's (1992) article stated that "only seldom has psychological peace research (sic) [...] found its way into psychology handbooks, let alone into textbooks" (p. 133), referencing only one exception, an entry by Kroner (1988). At the beginning of the 21st century, both the United States and Germany have seen the publication of a "handbook" of peace psychology with a distinguished publisher of academic psychological literature (Christie, Wagner, & Winter, 2001; Sommer & Fuchs, 2004).

In international psychology, peace psychology is in good standing. At the International Congress of Psychology in Acapulco in 1984, the International Union of Psychological Science (IUPsyS) explicitly rejected the inauguration of an ad hoc committee on the contributions of psychology to peace. The initiative came from a number of Eastern European delegates and was supported by a few "neutral" representatives. Four years later, at the next International Congress of Psychology in Sydney in 1988, a Committee for the Psychological Study of Peace (CPSP) was founded, albeit reluctantly, and Adolf Kossakowski, the President of the Psychological Association of the German Democratic Republic, was selected to be its chairman.

It is not an exaggeration to say that IUPsyS kept a jealous watch over the committee until the end of the cold war. This changed dramatically after 1991, once the cold war had ended. At that time Michael Wessells took over as chair of the CPSP.[1] Both he and the entire CPSP now were called upon by IUPsyS regularly to offer expertise on psychological aspects of war and peace. This was the case on the occasion of the Rwanda genocide and the Balkan wars and has continued ever since.

Last but not least, the inauguration in 1995 of the very journal in which this special issue appears is an indicator of the fact that since the early 1990s, peace psychology has come of age and no longer needs to hide under the wings of peace research as a specialty of political science.

But how has peace psychology fared in Germany? Details about the decades between the end of World War II and the end of the 1980s were reported by Boehnke (1992). This introduction to this special issue attempts to sketch the development of the last 20 years, that is, from the mid 1980s to the present day, though not without mentioning earlier efforts by political psychologists to put peace psychology on the agenda. A political psychology section of the German Association of Psychology Practitioners (Berufsverband Deutscher Psychologinnen und Psychologen) was founded as early as 1959 (Moser, 1979).

In Germany and other countries of Central Europe (West and East), the deployment of Soviet and U.S. missiles was a hot topic in the early and mid 1980s, bringing literally millions to the streets in protest. Psychologists participated in these protest actions in comparatively large numbers. In 1983, a Peace Initiative of Psychologists and the Psychosocial Professions was founded in West Germany, largely at the initiative of Anne Börner and Gert Sommer, the latter being the chair of the initiative until this year. It began by organizing large ad hoc conferences under the motto "Bewusst-Sein für den Frieden", which in German is a play on words, as "Bewusstsein (without the hyphen) für den Frieden" means "consciousness for peace", whereas "bewusst (new word) sein für den Frieden" means "to be consciously in favor of peace." In East Germany, psychologists in the Psychological Association of the German Democratic Republic founded a commission, "GDR-psychologists for peace and disarmament," in 1986. Adolf Kossakowski, and later Wolfgang Frindte from Friedrich Schiller University Jena, acted as chair. For a few years, this group was involved in the publication of a scientific journal named *Pro Pace Mundi* (ISSN 0232–3753). After the po-

---

[1]In 1999, Di Bretherton from Melbourne (Australia) became the chair of the CPSP; currently, Dan Christie from Ohio State University presides.

litical turn-about in East Germany, most of the members of this commission joined the West German peace initiative. A few years after German unification in 1990, the peace initiative changed its name to *Forum Friedenspsychologie* (Peace Psychology Forum). Since 1984, a newsletter of the peace initiative has appeared continuously, originally as an independent series but for the past decade as part of the scientific periodical *Wissenschaft und Frieden* [Science and Peace, ISSN 0947–3971], the journal with the largest circulation in the field. The organization currently has about 60 members, most of them very active. The first author of this article just took over as chair from founding president Gert Sommer.

In 1988, the group started to organize annual peace psychology conferences, which have taken place every year since. The year 2005 sees the 18th Annual Conference of Peace Psychology in Erlangen, organized by Christopher Cohrs. Often these conferences have served as an open forum for all kinds of peace psychology contributions. A number of the conferences had a special topic, such as "enemy images" (with Ralph White as a prominent speaker), "war and the media/peace journalism," "xenophobic crime," "human rights," "nonviolent conflict resolution," or the conflict potential of German unification. In recent years, the annual conference has opened itself more to the international scientific community by increasingly using English as its language of presentation. Two of the conferences were devoted to the preparation of *Krieg und Frieden: Handbuch der Konflikt- und Friedenspsychologie* [War and Peace: Handbook of Conflict and Peace Psychology] (Sommer & Fuchs, 2004). This 664-page handbook assembles 46 contributions, mostly by German peace psychologists, on diverse topics in three larger blocks (basic conceptual aspects, the culture of war, and forming the peace). A few U.S. colleagues also contributed to the volume (Daniel Druckman, Ronald Fisher, Michael Wessells, Daniel Christie, and Anne Anderson).

Also, outside of the "inner circle" of dedicated peace psychologists, the standing of Peace Psychology has greatly improved in the last 20 years. Although it was the case that in the 1980s peace psychologists had to combat the image of being mediocre scientists who substituted quality with partisanship, the very same colleagues have now become reputed evaluators of political psychology contributions to national psychology congresses, as well as members of editorial boards of scientific journals. Nowadays, contributions to national congresses are often solicited by the organizers, although in earlier years such contributions had a difficult time gaining acceptance to the program.

One grave problem, however, has meanwhile emerged. As mentioned, the central mobilizing event for German peace psychologists in the last 20 years was the political controversy around the deployment of Soviet and U.S. missiles in the mid 1980s. The activists of that time are now approaching retirement age, few being below 50 years of age. Only about 10% of the contributors to the peace psychology handbook are 35 or below. It is more than obvious that the German peace psychology guild has not been able to attract and educate successors for the field. Even though the reputation of peace psychology has undoubtedly grown in the years after the cold war, new blood is extremely scarce. Admittedly, there is no hot war and peace topic virulent in German public discourse at the moment but there also are structural reasons for the lack of new blood.

Peace psychology is not a discipline that allows young psychologists to make a career. This is true both for the job market and for academia. Even though the "Red scare" is no longer an impediment in the discipline, the closest professional field, that of political consultancy, clearly remains in the hands of political scientists, so that the job market for trained peace psychologists is narrow. In academia this is even truer. To earn an MA-equivalent degree in psychology in Germany, the so-called *Diplom*, all students at all public German universities[2] tend to go through one and the same type of academic curriculum. After all students have studied diverse basic subdisciplines of psychology in the BA-equivalent phase of their time at the university (general, social, developmental, personality, biological, and methods), the so-called *Grundstudium*, they specialize in two of three subdisciplines, namely in clinical psychology (most students choose this specialty), industrial and organizational psychology, or educational psychology, in the MA-equivalent phase of their studies, the *Hauptstudium*. Usually political psychology, let alone peace psychology, is not at all part of a German psychology program at any university. It remains a hobby of individual professors, not a structural option for young psychologists.

The situation has improved in graduate education (predominantly PhD studies) in recent years. In 2002, the *Deutsche Stiftung Friedensforschung*, the German Peace Research Foundation, was inaugurated by the federal government, securing a more continuous funding for peace research, including peace psychology projects. Furthermore, a number of graduate programs have been funded by diverse funding organizations, among them the *Deutsche Forschungsgemeinschaft*, a science funding organization similar to the National Science Foundation in the United States, which can, without much ado, be said to at least encompass peace psychology. Examples of such programs are the one headed by Amèlie Mummendey in Jena on "Conflict and Cooperation between Groups: Perspectives from Developmental and Social Psychology;" the programs for a Master in Peace Studies (University for Distance Education Hagen) or Peace and Conflict Studies (Philipps University Marburg), which are closely affiliated with a graduate program on "Group Related Misanthropy," headed by Ulrich Wagner and Wilhelm Heitmeyer; the Summer School on Peace and Conflict, organized by Gunter Bierbrauer at the University of Osnabrück; or the Peace Research Group at the University of Konstanz, headed by Wilhelm Kempf.

---

[2]German universities are almost exclusively public universities; the university of the issue editors is a rare exception.

All in all, peace psychology does continue to lead a niche existence. No degree in peace psychology on any academic level can be obtained from a German university, nor, for that matter, can one obtain a degree in political psychology.

Let us now turn to the contributions in this special issue. Altogether, there are six articles. The first five contributions are essentially quantitative in their research methodology; the final contribution by Ingrid I. Koop is a qualitative case study. Four of the six contributions are adaptations of contributions to *Forum Friedenspsychologie*'s 16th Annual Conference of Peace Psychology in Bremen in 2003; two were solicited for this special issue (Boehnke & Boehnke, and Frindte, Wettig, & Wammetsberger). These contributions have been selected from among 11 original submissions that were reviewed on the grounds of a long abstract. Needless to say, earlier drafts of the six selected contributions have, of course, been peer-reviewed by members of the editorial board of the journal, and additionally by experienced German reviewers.

The issue commences with an article by Wolfgang Frindte, Susan Wettig, and Dorit Wammetsberger from Friedrich Schiller University Jena titled "Old and New Anti-Semitic Attitudes in the Context of Authoritarianism and Social Dominance Orientation." It is not a matter of chance that this contribution is the inaugural contribution of the special issue on Peace Psychology in Germany. German anti-Semitism was at the core of the holocaust of European Jewry and has been a topic of permanent alert among German peace psychologists. The article by Frindte and his colleagues reports two studies on the psychological semantics of anti-Semitism. Old forms of anti-Semitism (explicit rejection of Jews) are contrasted with new forms of anti-Semitism, which come in the form of anti-Israeli attitudes and attitudes denying a special responsibility of the German people for the fate of Jews after the holocaust. The article also discusses the relationship between these two forms of anti-Semitism and personality syndromes like authoritarianism and a social dominance orientation.

The second article—by Jost Stellmacher and Gert Sommer from Philipps University Marburg, and Elmar Brähler from the University of Leipzig—is titled "Human Rights: Knowledge, Importance, and Support." Studies like the one presented by Stellmacher and his colleagues are rare cases in peace psychology, even from a global perspective, in that they work with representative samples. A major result of their studies is that knowledge about human rights is, in general, poor; and that it is even poorer when economic, social, and cultural rights are concerned than when civil and political rights are at stake. Only 1% of the German population has been actively engaged in human rights in the last 5 years. Stellmacher and colleagues found that knowledge about human rights increased feelings that human rights are important, and subjective importance fostered active engagement for human rights. They argue for an increase in human rights education as a prerequisite for improving the human rights situation in Germany (where, in particular, economic rights are a problem) and in other parts of the world.

The third article is authored by Christopher Cohrs from Friedrich-Alexander University Erlangen-Nürnberg, Barbara Moschner from Carl von Ossietzky University Oldenburg, Jürgen Maes from the University of the Armed Forces in Munich, and Sven Kielmann from the University of Trier. The article is titled "Personal Values and Attitudes Toward War." It reports two waves of a large German attitude survey. Personal values, as defined by the theory of basic human values by Schwartz (1992), ideological attitudes, threat of terrorism, and concern for human costs were taken into account. Militaristic attitudes were consistently related to a high priority of self-enhancement (power, achievement) and conservation (security, conformity) values and low priority of self-transcendence values (universalism, benevolence). Path analyses showed that the effects of conservation values were predominantly mediated by right-wing authoritarianism and threat of terrorism, yet the effects of self-enhancement and self-transcendence values were predominantly mediated by a social dominance orientation and a (lack of) concern for human costs. The authors conclude that two different psychological processes lead to support for war.

The fourth contribution to the issue comes from Michaela Kolbe and Margarete Boos, from the University of Göttingen, and Andrea Gurtner, who is now at the Université de Neuchatel in Switzerland after having spent some time at Göttingen. The article is titled "Social Identity in Times of International Conflict". It reports two studies on how young Europeans think about nationality, international conflict, and the impact on their social identity. One of the studies surveyed German high school students; the second included students from Spain, Switzerland, and Germany. In Spain, data gathering took place immediately after the terrorist attacks on Madrid commuter trains on March 11, 2004. Conceptually, the studies relied heavily on social identity theory (Tajfel & Turner, 1986) and self-categorization theory (Turner, Hogg, Oakes, Reicher, & Wetherell, 1987). The anticipated fears and personal changes in the event of war were manifold. Interpersonal influence by peers and social influence from reference groups as mediators of mass media are discussed as important factors in the development of social identity.

The fifth article is by Klaus Boehnke from the International University Bremen and Mandy Boehnke from the University of Bremen. It asks the question "Once a Peacenik—Always a Peacenik?" and offers an answer on the basis of a 6-wave, 19-year longitudinal study that was initiated in 1985, when participants were on average 14.5 years of age. Results indicate that the decisive predictor for political activism in middle adulthood is not so much early engagement in peace movement activities or a parental role model, but more what Inglehart (1977) labeled cognitive involvement. Values as defined by Inglehart, however, do not seem to be a good measure of cognitive involvement of adolescents. A much better predictor of long-term political engagement is the emotional, cognitive, and conative involvement with the political sphere. Youngsters who worry a lot about what goes on in the world; know a lot about "hot" political topics; and engage a lot in prepolitical behavior, such as discussing matters of political interest with their peers and their parents, are highly prone to become politically active adults, even if they do not engage in concrete political behavior in adolescence.

The final contribution comes from Ingrid Koop, a clinical psychologist from Bremen, who works in private practice and with "Refugio," a psychosocial center for traumatized refugees. Her article is titled "Refugees in Church Asylum: Psychological Peace Intervention Between Political Conflicts and Individual Suffering." She reports the case of a Kurdish refugee couple who stayed in church asylum in Germany for eight months. The personal history of the Kurdish refugees and the psychological interventions during their church asylum are described, and a brief overview of church asylum and its political and individual influence upon refugees is given. The article points out that a comprehensive understanding of church asylum can only be achieved if ethical (culture, religion, human rights), legal (legal representation, refugees' authorities, immigration authorities, courts), emotional (supporters' groups, friends, professionals), and public relations aspects (newspaper, radio, TV, events, public activities), as well as social (church community supporters, compatriots) and political (politicians, refugee and human rights groups) aspects of the problem, are discussed.

Taken together, the selection of articles makes clear that German peace psychology does not just have one focus, but that its topical interests are manifold. However, it also becomes clear that peace psychology in Germany tends to be an offspring of social psychology. Four of the six contributions to this special issue clearly have a social psychological thrust. Other foci are less frequent. In this issue one finds an article that is rooted in developmental psychology (Boehnke & Boehnke) and another one based in clinical and community psychology (Koop). A further important root of German peace psychology is, unfortunately, missing, namely that of media psychology and communication. Had it been possible to include such a contribution, one could even speak of a representative manifestation of the German peace psychology "landscape," a community clearly oriented towards social psychology, with some add-ons from developmental, clinical, and media psychology.

To sum up, we wish non-German readers, in particular, an inspiring reading experience that hopefully will lead to more networking between German peace psychologists and peace psychologists from the United States and other parts of the world.

BIOGRAPHICAL NOTES

Klaus Boehnke, born 1951, studied English, Russian, and Psychology, received a PhD in psychology from Berlin University of Technology in 1985, was assistant/associate professor, Department of Education, Free University of Berlin, was full Professor of Socialization Research, Department of Sociology, Chemnitz University of Technology, from 1993–2002, and since 2002 is a Professor of Social Science Methodology, International University Bremen. His research interests lie in the field of youth research and its methodology.

Daniel Fuss, born 1974, studied sociology, psychology, and political science. He received his MA in Sociology from Chemnitz University of Technology in 2000 and held positions of teaching assistant and lecturer at the Department of Sociology there. Since 2002, he is research associate in the EU funded project "Orientations of Young Men and Women Towards Citizenship and European Identity" at the International University Bremen. His research interests lie in the fields of identity research and social science methodology.

Angela Kindervater, born 1961, studied educational sciences, psychology, and sociology at the University of Hamburg. Her special interest is in authoritarianism and anti-Semitism. In 1990, she began working on several international projects in psychology, educational science, history, and public health. Since 2002, she is a research associate in a cross-cultural project on the political psychological consequences of the EU enlargement in 2004 at the International University Bremen.

REFERENCES

Boehnke, K. (1992). The status of psychological peace research in East and West Germany in a time of change. *Political Psychology, 13,* 133–144.

Christie, D. J., Wagner, R. V., & Winter, D. D. (2001). *Peace, conflict, and violence: Peace psychology for the 21st century.* Upper Saddle River, NJ: Prentice Hall.

Eberwein, W.-D., & Reichel, P. (1976). Friedens- und Konfliktforschung—Eine Einführung [Peace and Conflict Research—An Introduction]. Munich: Piper.

Inglehart, R. (1977). *The silent revolution.* Princeton, NJ: Princeton University Press.

Kroner, B. (1988). Friedensforschung [Peace research]. In R. Asanger & R. Wenninger (Eds.), *Handwörterbuch der Psychologie* (pp. 205–212). Munich: PVU.

Moser, H. (1979). Politische Psychologie [Political psychology]. Weinheim, Germany: Beltz.

Schwartz, S. H. (1992). Universals in the content and structure of values: Theoretical advances and empirical tests in 20 countries. *Advances in Experimental Social Psychology, 25,* 1–65.

Sommer, G., & Fuchs, A. (2004). Krieg und Frieden—Handbuch der Konflikt- und Friedenspsychologie [War and peace: Handbook of conflict and peace psychology]. Weinheim, Germany: BeltzPVU.

Tajfel, H., & Turner, J. C. (1986). The social identity theory of intergroup behavior. In S. Worchel & W. G. Austin (Eds.), *Psychology of intergroup relations* (pp. 7—24). Chicago: Nelson-Hall.

Turner, J. C., Hogg, M. A., Oakes, P. J. Reicher, S. D., & Wetherell, M. S. (1987). *Rediscovering the social group: A self-categorization theory.* Cambridge, MA: Basil Blackwell.

"Over and over, we have observed that actions motivated by the desire for punishment produce retaliation from the other side, and that actions motivated by a desire for peace produce acts of peace from the other side ... real safety and peace can be achieved, despite enormous odds, only when people are able to see the 'humanity' of those who attack them ... empathizing with the fears, hurt, rage and unmet human needs that are behind the attacks."

Marshall Rosenberg,
Center for Nonviolent Communication;
statement issued September 27, 2001

PEACE AND CONFLICT: JOURNAL OF PEACE PSYCHOLOGY, *11*(3), 239–266

Old and New Anti-Semitic Attitudes in the Context of Authoritarianism and Social Dominance Orientation— Two Studies in Germany

Wolfgang Frindte
Friedrich Schiller University, Jena, Germany

Susan Wettig
University of Erfurt, Germany

Dorit Wammetsberger
Friedrich Schiller University, Jena, Germany

On the basis of a new heuristic model of anti-Semitism, researchers are able to distinguish between new and old aspects of anti-Semitic attitudes. The results of two studies suggest that anti-Semitism in Germany contains very different aspects and the data fit the new theoretical model. Both traditional aspects, like "manifest anti-Semitism," as well as new forms of anti-Semitic attitudes, like "latent anti-Semitism," "rejection of responsibility for Jews," "anti-Israeli attitudes," and "anti-Zionism," were found. Furthermore, we identified various anti-Semitic attitudes with different predictive elements. Individuals with extreme anti-Semitic attitudes differ significantly from those without anti-Semitic attitudes with regard to the extent of authoritarianism, readiness for violence, approval of the repetition of National Socialism, and political orientation. The comparison between the two general concepts, authoritarianism and social dominance orientation, demonstrated that authoritarianism has greater utility in explaining separate aspects of old and new anti-Semitic attitudes. The implications of these findings are discussed.

Correspondence should be sent to Wolfgang Frindte, Friedrich Schiller University, Jena, Department of Psychology, Unit of Communication Psychology, Am Steiger 3/ Haus 1, 07743 Jena, Germany. E-mail: wolfgang.frindte@uni-jena.de

Almost 60 years after the end of World War II and the National Socialist geno-cide of European Jews, the relationship between Germans and Jews is still char-acterized by tension. A new public debate about Germany's history, the Holo-caust, and responsibility is emerging. Paul Spiegel, the leader of Germany's Jewish community, said, "What changed, however, is the openness in respect to the expression of *anti-Semitism* today … . Many anti-Semites considered it to be inopportune to expose their anti-Semitism 10 years ago. Today, they express it" (*Die Zeit*, 2001, p. 25).

There are only 100,000 Jews living in Germany today, compared to 80 million non-Jews. The treatment of Jewish citizens in Germany can be seen as an indicator of group relations between minorities and majorities within German society. This implies that not only do conflicts between Germans and Jews represent the way minorities are generally treated in Germany but also that the underlying causes of such conflicts, as well as the solutions proposed to remedy such conflicts, are typi-cal. Hence, conflict between Jews and non-Jews in Germany qualifies as a relevant issue for peace research.

THEORETICAL BACKGROUND

Anti-Semitism in Germany—Change in Social Attitudes

According to Henryk M. Broder, "there is anti-Semitism not despite, but because of Auschwitz, because the perpetrators and their inheritors are permanently re-minded of their atrocities and of their failure at the same time. Each living and sur-viving Jew is a witness and reproach at the same time" (Broder, 1986, S.11). The Holocaust stands as a model for the prevailing majority's way of dealing with "for-eign" minorities. As Dahmer (1993) stated, dealing with "foreign" people in Eu-rope was first practiced when interacting with the Jews.

Anti-Semitism reflects the negative stereotypes by which non-Jews try to de-fame the Jews as Jews (Frindte, Funke & Jacob, 1999; Horkheimer & Adorno, 1944). The forms of such defamation have changed since the end of Nazism (e.g., Bergmann & Erb, 2000; Eisinga, Konig & Scheepers, 1995; Gibson & Duch, 1992; Raden, 1993; T. W. Smith, 1993). The purpose of this article is to illustrate some of these changes from a psychological perspective.

Anti-Semitism in Germany has caused problems both within society and with regards to the examination of its underlying causal factors, its development, and its impact since the end of the Third Reich. The difficulty and complexity of the scien-tific analysis of this phenomenon is caused by events that occurred during the pe-riod of National Socialism and the effects of these events into the present.

Scientific research on anti-Semitism in Germany observes the emergence of a "secondary anti-Semitism," which distances itself from the Holocaust and considers the past closed. This modern hostility against Jews is linked to a public taboo regarding the past. That interaction may bring about new forms of anti-Semitic attitudes and the possible destabilization of German society. The prior research on anti-Semitic attitudes has established the necessity of a differentiated view of the phenomenon of anti-Semitism, including a consideration of its links to relevant historical, social, and individual elements. Bergmann & Erb (2000) referred to the fact that the large number of investigations conducted in Germany since 1986 have all discovered an association between anti-Semitic attitudes and a particular demographic group, in that persons expressing negative attitudes towards Jews belong to the generation that experienced National Socialism, have a low educational level, and regard themselves as both right-wing politically and as nationalists. This pattern appears to have changed and to have become more complex since the middle of the 1990s.

It is assumed that anti-Jewish attitudes are linked to a specific perception of history and current political changes. First, Sturzbecher & Freytag (2000) reached the conclusion that there are particular characteristics that distinguish anti-Semitic attitudes from "ordinary" prejudices. Anti-Jewish attitudes involve a special historical continuity, even though their contents have changed over centuries and have adapted to the respective "zeitgeist." Furthermore, compared to prejudices against other minorities, the contents of resentments against Jews are usually strongly related to one another. In the special discourse of German anti-Semitism research, the phenomenon is generally regarded as an independent attitude complex with a distinct motive structure mainly determined by National Socialism (e.g., Bergmann & Erb, 1991; Frindte, Funke & Jacob, 1997; Frindte, Wammetsberger & Wettig, 2003; Heitmeyer, 2003). Second, anti-Semitism seems to be a private prejudice without ideological basis, but with a strong political power (Marin, 1980). On the one hand, open expressions of anti-Semitic attitudes are described as individual cases, as statements only voiced in privacy behind locked doors. On the other hand, political scandals and debates in Germany show that anti-Jewish prejudices are still prominent in public discourses in the country of the perpetrators of anti-Semitic activities (e.g., Kindervater, 2004). For example, the description of the Jewish people as "people of perpetrators"—"Taetervolk"—in a speech on the German Day of Reunification in October, 2003, by member of Parliament Martin Hohmann; or the debate about the memorial for the murdered European Jews. Third, and most important within the context of this article, current studies on anti-Semitic attitudes increasingly indicate the existence of evidence of a persisting latent anti-Semitism among Germans. The prevalence of prejudice against Jews is evident in statements such as "Jews have too much power in Germany and the world" and "Jews make use of the Holocaust" (Wittenberg & Schmidt, 2003). For instance, an opinion poll supported by the American Jewish Committee shows that in 2002, 63.7% of 2319 German adults agreed with the statement "Jews make use of the Holocaust," and 51.5 % agreed with the item "Jews have too much power

in the world" (Wittenberg & Schmidt, 2003). Fourth, traditional anti-Semitic attitudes and criticism of the policy of Israel seem to form a volatile combination. The
latest report on "Manifestations of anti-Semitism in the EU 2002—2003" (EUMC,
2004) discussed the empirical basis of new anti-Semitism "as anti-Zionism or as
critique of Israel, or behind anti-ideologies such as anti-racism or anti-imperial-
ism" (EUMC, 2004, p. 24). The rise in the number of anti-Semitic incidents in Germany over the last years and a simultaneous increase in anti-Israeli feelings in Germany could indicate a connection between anti-Semitism and exaggerated
criticism of Israel. In 1993, the German Federal Office for Internal Security reported 649 criminal acts of an anti-Semitic nature. In 2002, 1334 criminal acts with
an anti-Semitic background were registered (http://www.verfassungsschutz.de/
news). At the same time, a recent Eurobarometer survey (an opinion poll in 15
countries of the European Union) showed that nearly 59% of Europeans and 65%
of Germans thought that Israel presented a threat to world peace (Eurobarometer,
2003).

AUTHORITARIANISM AND SOCIAL DOMINANCE
ORIENTATION AS PREDICTORS FOR ANTI-SEMITISM

In the field of xenophobic prejudice research, and in German research into
anti-Semitism in particular, the concept of authoritarianism has played an important role for decades (Adorno, Frenkel-Brunswik, Levinson, & Sanford, 1950;
Altemeyer, 1998; Funke, 2002; Rippl, Seipel, & Kindervater, 2000; Wagner, van
Dick, & Zick, 2001; Weiss, 1999). The book "The Authoritarian Personality" was
followed by over 2,000 scientific publications on authoritarianism (Meloen, 1991)
and manifold theoretical and empirical innovations (e.g., Altemeyer, 1996;
Duckitt, 1992; Duckitt, Wagner, du Plessis & Birum, 2002; Duncan, Peterson, &
Winter, 1997; Lederer & Schmidt, 1995; McFarland, Ageyev, & Abalakina, 1993;
Oesterreich, 1996; Six, Wolfradt, & Zick, 2001; A. G. Smith & Winter, 2002;
Stone, Lederer, & Christie, 1993).

The key assumption of authoritarianism is that the political and social attitudes
of the individual are based on a psychological structure characterized by Ego
weakness, aggressiveness, and hostile behavior in relation to outgroups. Despite
subsequent criticism of the applied psychodynamic concept and of the empirical
procedure utilized by Adorno et al. (1950), elements of the Authoritarianism Scale
(F-Scale) are of major importance in the research on authoritarianism and
anti-Semitism. Altemeyer (1988, 1996), argued on the basis of his theory of
Right-Wing Authoritarianism (RWA) that right-wing authoritarianism is an individual difference variable, a personal trait developed on the premise that some people need little situational pressure to submit to authority and attack others; however
others require significantly more (Altemeyer, 1996, p. 8). He defined *RWA* as an

individual factor, as a personality construct, or "a 'trait' if you like" (Altemeyer, 1988, p. 3), which manifests in three attitude clusters: authoritarian submission, authoritarian aggressiveness, and conventionalism.

The relationship between authoritarian attitudes and xenophobic hostileness is widely documented in the academic literature. For example, Altemeyer (1988, 1998) suggested substantial links between RWA and discriminatory attitudes towards Arabs, Asians, and African Americans. Correlations between authoritarianism and anti-Semitic attitudes, already evident in early studies on Authoritarian Personality (Adorno et al., 1950), were re-examined a decade ago in a representative sample of white, non-Jewish, North Americans by Raden (1993). Although earlier investigations in the United States (Martire & Clark, 1982; Selznick & Steinberg, 1969) interpreted anti-Semitism as a part of a general authoritarian syndrome, the General Social Survey conducted by Raden in 1988 indicated that self-reported negative affects against Jews are not related to a conservative-authoritarian attitude syndrome. Yet, Lederer and Kindervater (see Lederer & Schmidt, 1995) were able to persuasively demonstrate such connections between anti-Semitic attitudes and authoritarianism, ethnocentrism, attitudes to the public authority, and attitudes to politics and school in an Austrian study. There does, therefore, seem to be empirical evidence for the close relationship between anti-Semitism and authoritarianism.

In contrast to the RWA, the Social Dominance Theory (SDT; see Sidanius & Pratto, 1993, 1999), which has become increasingly popular since the end of the 1980s, provides a more complex explanation of xenophobic attitudes and social discriminations. Sidanius and Pratto (1999) assumed that conflicts within a society are determined to a considerable extent by social hierarchies resulting from group membership. The SDT differentiates between three systems used for group-based hierarchy formation: the age system; the gender system; and an arbitrary system that employs characteristics such as skin color, religion, and sexual orientation for the arrangement of groups. To stabilize these hierarchies, legitimating myths or ideologies are put to use, which are shared by the population in the form of attitudes, values, attribution, or beliefs. The individual cognitive manifestation of these myths or ideologies in a particular person is designated as that person's Social Dominance Orientation (SDO). Individuals with a strong SDO judge other humans on the basis of their group status and argue that some groups are better or of more worth than others (Sidanius & Pratto, 1999). The SDO has gained acceptance as a predictor of discriminatory attitudes in the psychological research of prejudice during recent years. This development stems from the theoretical necessity to combine individual discrimination tendencies based on hierarchical social structures with intergroup processes.

Sidanius and Pratto (1999) considered their theoretical conceptions to be confirmed by various empirical investigations. Their SDO-Scale has a high degree of internal consistency, with an alpha of not less than .80 (Duriez & van Hiel, 2002;

Levin, Federico, Sidanius, & Rabinowitz, 2002; Sidanius & Pratto, 1999; Whitley, 1999; for adapted versions of the scale see Six et al., 2001, and Zachariae, 2003). Gender was also determined to be a stable covariate of SDO (Sidanius, Pratto, & Bobo, 1994; see also Lippa & Arad, 1999). In addition, relationships between SDO and individual personality characteristics have been revealed (Pratto, Sidanius, Stallworth, & Malle, 2001; Sidanius & Pratto, 1999; Zachariae, 2003). Likewise, high levels of SDO are associated with a range of hierarchy promoting social ideologies. In particular, associations between SDO and political–economic conservatism and sexism, nationalism, and patriotism ought to be emphasized (Sidanius & Pratto, 1999).

The remarkable predictive qualities of both RWA and SDO with regard to ethnocentric and xenophobic attitudes raise the question of similarities and differences between these concepts. On the one hand, Six et al. (2001) characterized RWA and SDO as generalized attitudes, according to the definition by Allport (1935). Such generalized attitudes should not be understood as specific to individuals (Six et al., 2001, p. 24; cf. also Allport, 1935). On the other hand, Altemeyer (1998) and Sidanius and Pratto (1999) stressed the conceptual autonomy of both concepts. The authoritarian personality is described as being submissive to authorities of the ingroup that defends the values of that group. In contrast, "social dominators" discriminate against outgroups due to a perceived inferiority in relation to their own group: "Still, *most* social dominators do not belong to the 'RWA Club'" (Altemeyer, 1988, p. 62). Therefore, authoritarianism involves intragroup relations, and SDO is primarily based on intergroup relations. Empirical studies confirm the differences of these constructs. Most studies demonstrate only small to medium correlations between RWA and SDO (e.g., Altemeyer, 1998; Duckitt, Wagner, du Plessis, & Birum, 2002; Duriez & van Hiel, 2002; Heaven & Connors, 2001; Petzold, 2004; Sidanius & Pratto, 1999; Six et al., 2001; Zachariae, 2003).

The Relation Between RWA, SDO, and Anti-Semitic Attitudes

The differences between RWA and SDO suggest they are able to explain different forms of hostile attitudes towards foreigners. However, the empirical findings are ambiguous. Van Hiel & Mervielde (2002) concluded that RWA and SDO predict xenophobia and racism in student samples to the same extent. In nonstudent samples, however, SDO proved to be a slightly better predictor. The results of Lippa and Arad (1999) and Duckitt et al. (2002) showed that both RWA and SDO are useful explanatory concepts in the analysis of prejudices. However, they were also able to detect slight differences in the predictive strength of both constructs. Authoritarianism seems to be somewhat better able to predict nationalistic ways of thinking, with SDO being more informative with regards to generalized resentment in relation to foreigner's groups. In summary, as concluded by Six et al.

(2001) and Funke (2002), RWA and SDO are best understood as different constructs of generalized attitudes. SDO is the more modern and complex attitude
construct (Petzold, 2004). Nevertheless, it appears that both RWA and SDO are
particularly relevant in explaining anti-Semitic attitudes in Germany: Modern German anti-Semitism could also be understood as an exclusively ideological complex, which needs neither social conflict nor the existence of Jewish population for
its justification. In this case, the group or environment affiliation would be of less
importance for the development of anti-Semitic attitudes, as these would depend
on certain personality structures (cognitive abilities, authoritarianism, etc.;
Bergmann & Erb, 2000). Furthermore, it has to be stated that the role of social factors in causing anti-Semitism is becoming increasingly less clear.
Sociodemographic and other social anti-Semitic attitude variables have less explanatory power than they had in anti-Semitism research of earlier decades.

Research Questions

We assume that anti-Semitism and the rejection of a historical responsibility for
Jews in Germany are closely related. Furthermore, the communication of anti-Semitic attitudes is subjected to public censorship. As a result, criticism of Israel and
anti-Zionism could represent special forms of substituted communication of
anti-Semitic attitudes, and thus could be described as modern forms or derivations
of anti-Semitism. Because authoritarianism, and in recent times SDO as well, are
discussed in the research literature as predictors for the development or maintenance of Xenophobia (and concomitantly anti-Semitic attitudes), out studies will
also investigate the influence of these constructs on anti-Semitic prejudices. We
are particularly interested in determining differences in the effects RWA and SDO
have on different aspects of anti-Semitic attitudes. To study the structure and the
relations of anti-Semitic attitudes, we constructed a heuristic model of anti-Semitism. A first version of this model consisted of three components of possible
anti-Jewish attitudes, namely *manifest anti-Semitism*, *latent anti-Semitism* and the
rejection of responsibility for Jews. Manifest anti-Semitism describes the "classic
anti-Semitism" of regarding Jews as Jews, and includes references to the Jewish
infiltration of society, to religious motivation of anti-Semitic attitudes and to the
aggressive exclusion of the Jews. Latent anti-Semitism contains two aspects: first,
a subtle and diffuse antipathy against Jews and second, the phenomenon that some
individuals do not express their negative attitudes about Jews publicly (Bergmann
& Erb, 1997). Rejection of responsibility for Jews refers to the demand for
"Schlusstrich," an end to discussion of the past, along with the concomitant demand for a "normal" relationship with Jews and Israel, and a strong rejection of
feelings of guilt. This model formed the theoretical basis for the first study.
  Against the background of the new debates about anti-Jewish prejudices since
2000 (mentioned previously) we developed an extended version of the first model

with two further components: *exaggerated Israel criticism* and *anti-Zionism*. Exaggerated Israel criticism is directed to the policy of Israel in the Middle-East conflict, in which Israel is seen as the evil in the Middle East, and as a "Nazi country" attacking "defenseless Palestinians." Examples of indicators of exaggerated Israel criticism are the description of the behavior of the Israeli troops against Palestinians as "Nazi-methods," or the comparison of the Israeli Prime Minister Sharon with Hitler. Anti-Zionism is a movement against the establishment of, and support for, a national homeland for Jews in Middle East. Anti-Zionist attitudes are opposed to the Jewish state's right to exist in Israel (see Freedland, 2003, p. 119). This extended model was used in a second study.

The empirical analyses presented in this article focused on five main research questions. First, does the public avoidance of expressing anti-Semitic statements and the refusal of further discussions about German fault and responsibility for the Jewish people constitute a new aspect of anti-Semitic attitudes? Second, if they do, to what extent are these new aspects of anti-Semitic attitudes linked to general hostility towards foreigners? Third, are there individual or social conditions that could serve as predictors of anti-Semitic attitudes? Fourth, how are exaggerated Israel criticism and anti-Zionism related to anti-Semitism? Finally, are there any differences between the two theoretical concepts of authoritarianism and SDO with regard to the explanation of old and new aspects of anti-Semitism?

METHOD

Study 1

To answer the first three research questions, a field study examined the three-component model of anti-Semitism and the effects of authoritarianism, hostility towards foreigners, political orientation, and other sociostructural variables on the prediction of several anti-Semitic attitudes.

Subjects

In this study, 2,130 young people (14 to 18 years old, randomly selected from various Federal States of Germany) in Germany were asked to complete a standardized questionnaire. Randomly selected participants completed the questionnaire either on university campus, at several public places, or at home.

Assessment of Variables

The questionnaire comprised different scales and a number of single items: a three-dimensional anti-Semitism-scale consisting of 12 items, for example

- "I don't like Jews." (manifest anti-Semitism)
- "I do not talk to just anyone about Jews." (latent anti-Semitism)
- "Decades after the end of the war, we should not talk so much about the Holocaust. We should close the discussions about the past." (rejection of responsibility for Jews; reliability of the scale, α = .88)
- A one-dimensional scale to measure attitudes towards foreigners (consisting of 9 items, e.g., "Foreigners in Germany should not push themselves into situations where they are not welcome." α = .87)
- Acceptance of violence (9 items, e.g., "Violence is a justified means to assert political interests." α = .64)
- Readiness for violence (5 items, e.g., "I am willing to assert my own interests by force." α = .73)
- A short version of Altemeyer's (1988) one-dimensional RWA Scale (containing 5 items, e.g., "What we need in our country is a good deal of law and order instead of more civil rights." α = .76)

Moreover, we investigated the individual's political orientation ("Left-Right Self-anchoring Scale") and approval of the repetition of National Socialism by means of single items (for all items and scales, see Appendix).

Results

Regarding the first and most important research question, analyses indicate a three-dimensional structure of anti-Semitism, with the data fitting the theoretical model.[1] The results of a factor-analysis supports the theoretical 3-dimension-structure of anti-Semitic orientation. The analysis of the main components (with varimax-rotation) supported the three factors, which altogether explain 62.7% of the variance: Factor I (43.5%) contains all the items describing manifest anti-Semitism; Factor II (10.7%) refers to common traits of the three items in the rejection of responsibility for Jewish people subscale; Factor III (8.6%) incorporates items in the latent anti-Semitism subscale. In confirmatory factor-analysis, the three-component-structure with correlating factors was also supported by the structural equation modeling approach set up using LISREL (Lineral Structural Relationships, see also Jöreskog, Sörbom, du Toit, & du Toit, 1999). Further, a one-factor-model (without differentiation between the three sub-dimensions) proved to be significantly worse than the three-factor-model with correlating sub-dimensions. Table 1 lists items in our anti-Semitism-Scale and their factor affiliations.

---

[1]In further empirical studies between 1996 and 2002, we used these three components as a basic model to describe new aspects of anti-Semitism. We changed substantial contents of the model and supplemented a fourth aspect in 2003.

TABLE 1
Study 1—Anti-Semitism Scale Items

Item	Factor Affiliations
It's better for Germany to have no Jews at all.	.824
The Jews in Germany have too much influence.	.789
The Jews have too much influence over the world.	.777
I don't like Jews.	.819
The Jews should not hold higher positions in the government.	.702
One should not interact with Jews.	.780
The German people must take a special responsibility for the Jews.	.560
As a young person in Germany I don't have to be responsible for the Jews.	.799
Decades after the end of the war, we should not talk so much about the Holocaust. We should close the discussions about the past.	.810
I think that many people do not reveal their true opinion about Jews.	.704
The subject "Jew" is an unpleasant thing for me.	.583
I do not talk to just anyone about Jews.	.700

To answer the second question, a confirmatory factor-analysis was computed (with help from LISREL). The items of the anti-Semitism and "hostility toward foreigners" scales were included in the analysis. Altogether, three models were tested, and the last model (see Figure 1) proved to be superior to the other two. All three dimensions of anti-Semitism are strongly related to hostility toward foreigners, and manifest anti-Semitism is especially strongly related.

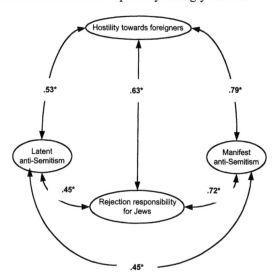

FIGURE 1   Statistical structural model. Note: Hostility toward foreigners, manifest anti-Semitism, latency of anti-Semitism, and rejection of responsibility for Jews; ($\chi^2 = 1707.833$; $df = 223$; $p = 0.000$; RMSEA = 0.056; CFI = 0.982; GFI = 0.984).

TABLE 2
Predictors for the Three Dimensions of the Anti-Semitism Model
(Multiple Regression-Analysis)

Predictors	Manifest Anti-Semitism		Latent Anti-Semitism		Rejection of Responsibility for the Jews	
	β	Significance	β	Significance	β	Significance
Authoritarianism	.357	.000	.366	.000	.215	.000
Political orientation (right/left wing)	.159	.000				
Readiness for violence	.253	.000	.153	.000	.149	.000
Agreement to the repetition of the national-socialism	.189	.000				
R^2	.493		.202		.151	
Adjusted R^2	.492		.201		.149	

A multiple regression analysis answered the third question about the predictors of the three dimensions of anti-Semitic attitudes (see Table 2).[3] Manifest anti-Semitic attitudes are anchored in an authoritarian, violence-supporting, traditional, and right-orientated political value system, as well as in approval of historic National Socialism. Only authoritarianism and the support of violence have a significant influence on the latent communication of anti-Semitism and rejection of responsibility for Jews. However, neither dimensions are connected with positive attitudes regarding National Socialism nor with specific right-orientated political orientations. We hypothesize that latency of anti-Semitism and the rejection of responsibility for Jews are parts of a common attitude among most young people, and provide a picture of reactions to everyday culture in Germany.

This demonstrates that our new model of anti-Semitism could be a useful tool to improve the understanding of the relationship between an old-fashioned stereotype and its newer manifestations.

STUDY 2

In 2003, a second field study examined the extended component model of anti-Semitism and the effect of authoritarianism and social dominance orientation on the prediction of several anti-Semitic attitudes. Although both manifest and latent anti-Semitic attitudes reflect fundamental negative prejudices against Jews,

---

[3]The variables *education* and *age* showed significant influence on anti-Semitic attitudes. A higher educational level is correlated with weaker anti-Semitism, whereas a higher age is positive correlated with anti-Semitism.

they are at the same time qualitatively different and should be kept separate from one other, whereas the rejection of responsibility for Jewish people is assumed to constitute a modern form of anti-Semitic resentments. Whether and when anti-Zionism and exaggerated Israel criticism is to be regarded as anti-Semitism is an open question in public debates. Hence, we extended our model with two further components. One of these components is called *exaggerated anti-Israeli attitudes* and is operationalized with items like "Palestinian suicidal attacks on Israelis are the right instruments to fight against Israel" or "Israelis are an occupying power and they have no business to be in Palestine." The other additional component is called *anti-Zionist attitudes* and is operationalized with items like "The foundation of the state of Israel was a mistake" or "It would be better, if the Jews would go away from the Middle East." We assumed that both RWA and SDO offer valuable, but distinguishable, constructs to explain anti-Semitic subdimensions.

Subjects and Procedure

Four hundred and eleven participants between the age of 18 and 83 (average 40.28 years) in Baden-Wuerttemberg, Bavaria, Lower Saxony, Saxony, and Thuringia (Germany) were surveyed. Fifty-eight percent of the participants were women, 42% were men. Their educational level covers secondary school (57%), elementary school (30%), and extended elementary school (5%). In total, 40% of the participants reported the possession of an academic degree or that they work in an academic field.

The investigation was conducted from December 2002 until March 2003. Participants were provided with a booklet containing questions concerning different aspects of the role of the Jews in German society and the political conflict between Israel and Palestine. To reduce socially desirable answers, anonymity was guaranteed and maintained. Randomly selected participants completed the questionnaire either on university campus, at several public places, or at home before sending the questionnaires back to the university.

Assessment of Variables

The procedure for assessing authoritarianism differed from that employed in Study 1, as the RWA³D-Scale from Funke (2002)—which consists of 12 items that are equally subdivided between the dimensions "authoritarian aggression," "authoritarian submission," and "conventionalism"—was used. For the SDO-Scale, a translation of the 16-item version by Six et al. (2001) was used. The scale is internally consistent, with a Cronbach's α of .82. In addition, we employed a "Left-Right Self-anchoring Scale" to measure the political orientation of the participants on a 5-point Likert-type scale ranging from 1 (*left*) to 5 (*right*).

A new and advanced anti-Semitic-Scale ($\alpha = .91$) was composed, on the basis of the first study's results, as well as research conducted by Bergmann and Erb (1991), Enyedi (1999), Frindte et al. (1999), Kovács (1999a, 1999b), Pettigrew and Meertens (1995), T. W. Smith (1993), and Sturzbecher and Freytag (2000). Some new items were developed by Petzold (2004; see Table 3 and Appendix). The subscale manifest anti-Semitism is composed of 10 classic anti-Semitism items. The subscale latent anti-Semitism consists of nine items. Manifest and latent anti-Semitism items were subsequently combined to form one scale, and demonstrated a satisfying level of internal reliability ($\alpha = .90$). The scale rejection of responsibility for Jews ($\alpha = .80$) contains six items. In addition, 5 items inquired about exaggerated anti-Israeli attitudes ($\alpha = .79$) and four items represent the component "anti-Zionist attitudes" ($\alpha = .60$). After several exploratory factor-analyses, the original number of items in each scale was reduced (see the following).

Results

To address the fourth research question, data were analyzed in several exploratory and confirmatory factor-analysis (LISREL; Scientific Software International, 2004). So as to be consistent with the aims of the study, we tried to discern the structure of anti-Semitism by using exploratory factor-analyses (main component analyses including varimax-rotation). Four components were extracted, which explain 60.02 % of the variance. The results of these analyses and the items with high and clear factor-loadings are illustrated in Table 3.

Figure 2 shows the result of a confirmatory factor-analysis (with help from LISREL; Scientific Software International, 2004), which illustrates the relations between the various components of anti-Jewish attitudes. The items of the anti-Semitism scales were included in this analysis. Altogether, three-, four- and five-component models were tested and the following four-component-model (see also Table 4) proved to be superior to the others. All four dimensions of anti-Semitism (exaggerated criticism of Israel, anti-Zionism, and the traditional and modern forms of anti-Semitism) are strongly interrelated.

To test the fifth research question concerning the differences between the theoretical concepts of RWA and SDO, with regard to their ability to explain the old and new aspects of anti-Semitism, the data were fitted to a structural equation model (LISREL). As evident in the model (see Figure 3), the previous four components of anti-Semitism and their derivations are implemented as endogenous variables. Through the specification of the exogenous variables, the contribution of RWA, SDO, and Left-Right-Orientation (LRO) to anti-Semitism was tested. The model presented in the following obtained the highest indexes of fit (GFI = .94, CFI = .98). RWA loaded relatively high on manifest/latent anti-Semitism ($\lambda = .45$) and significantly, although marginally lower, on rejection of responsibility for Jews ($\lambda = .26$) and anti-Israel attitudes ($\lambda = .22$). The regression coefficient

TABLE 3
Study 2- Anti-Semitism Scale Items

	Factor 1 "Manifest & Latent Anti-Semitism"	Factor 2 "Anti-Israeli Attitudes"	Factor 3 "Rejection of Responsibility for the Jews"	Factor 4 Anti-Zionism
One should avoid having business dealings with Jews.	.747			
One should not interact with Jews.	.810			
I don't like Jews.	.768			
It's better for Germany to have no Jews at all.	.760			
The Jews should not hold higher positions in the government.	.725			
The Jews in Germany have too much influence.	.675			
Marriages between Jews and non-Jews should be avoided.	.674			
Jews living here should not push themselves where they are not wanted.	.727			
The subject "Jew" is an unpleasant thing for me.	.571			
Jews teach their children values and skills different from those required to be successful in Germany.	.569			
Decades after the end of the war, we should not talk so much about the Holocaust. We should close the discussions about the past.			.764	
One should finally stop the discussion about our guilt towards the Jews.			.826	
The foundation of the state Israel was a mistake.				.771
Israel is solely responsible for the development and maintenance of the conflicts in the Middle East.		.726		
Israel is a state which stops at nothing.		.723		
Israel starts wars and blames others for it.		.791		
Israelis are illegitimate occupiers of the Palestinian areas.		.748		
It would be better if the Jews would leave the Middle East.				.617
The way Israelis deal with Palestinians is similar to what Nazi Germany did to the Jews.		.594		

Note. Four-dimensional factor solution of the anti-Semitism Scale, loadings < 0.3 were suppressed. Explanation of variation: Factor 1 (26.95%): "manifest/latent anti-Semitism;" Factor 2 (15.69%): "exaggerated anti-Israeli attitudes;" Factor 3 (11.39%): "rejection of responsibility for Jewish people;" Factor 4 (6.35%): "anti-Zionist attitudes."

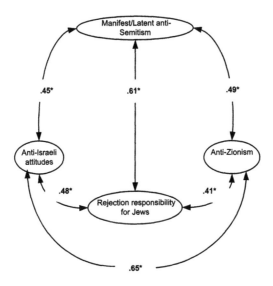

FIGURE 2   Statistical structural model. Satorra-Bentler Scaled χ^2 = 51.32; df = 38 (p = 0.07304); Normal Theory Weighted Least Squares χ^2 = 72.49; df = 38 (p = 0.00063); RMSEA = 0.030; CFI = 0.99; GFI = 0.97.

from RWA to anti-Zionist attitudes is not significant. Moreover, the effects of SDO on all endogenous variables (components of anti-Jewish attitudes) did not achieve significance. A Pearson's correlational analysis detected a relationship between RWA and SDO of a similar magnitude to previous research findings (λ = .42, p = .001).[4] The negative significant effect of LRO on anti-Israel attitudes (λ = -.27) indicates that left-orientated participants are particularly motivated to voice their anti-Zionist attitudes. However, the error-variances of the components of anti-Jewish attitudes on the right side of the model indicate that there are further unknown variables exerting a strong influence on anti-Semitic attitudes and their derivations.

DISCUSSION

Our data suggest that even more than 55 years after the Holocaust, anti-Semitism in Germany is still a very distinct phenomena. Some substantial conclusions can be drawn from these explorations of new types of anti-Semitism. The first study dem-

---

[4]The variables *age* and *sex* showed a significant influence on anti-Semitic attitudes. Men and older people are more likely to be anti-Semitic than women and younger people. The effect of education is not significant.

TABLE 4
Fit Indexes of the Structural Equation Modeling with Three, Four and Five
Components of Anti-Semitic Statements

Models	Satorra-Bentler χ^2	RMSEA	CFI	GFI
Three-component model	88.20	.054	.98	.94
Four-component model	51.32	.030	.99	.97
Five-component model	52.42	.055	.93	.94

Note.   Satorra-Bentler Scaled χ^2 (Satorra & Bentler, 1999); RMSEA = Root Mean Square Error of Approximation; CFI = Comparative Fit Index; GFI = Goodness of Fit Index.

onstrates that the model with three components of possible anti-Jewish attitudes (manifest anti-Semitism, latent anti-Semitism, and the rejection of responsibility for Jews) could be a useful tool to improve the understanding of the relationship between an old-fashioned stereotype and its newer manifestations. All three dimensions of anti-Semitism are strongly related to hostility towards foreigners—manifest anti-Semitism is especially strongly associated. If, in Germany, young people today share anti-Semitic opinions, then it may mostly be in conjunction with general hostility towards foreigners. Anti-Semitism after Auschwitz among youth is not an anti-Semitism without objects. These objects, however, seem to be not only Jews, but also strangers and foreigners in general. Therefore,

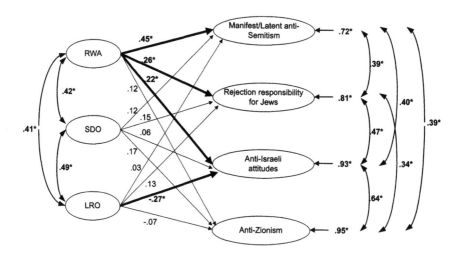

FIGURE 3   Manifest and latent anti-Semitism, rejection of responsibility for Jews, anti-Israeli attitudes, and anti-Zionism; Satorra-Bentler Scaled χ^2 = 136.12; df = 84 (p = 0.00028); Normal Theory Weighted Least Squares χ^2 = 201.79; df = 84 (p = 0.00000); RMSEA = 0.040; CFI = 0.98; GFI = 0.94. The paths from RWA to anti-Zionism, from SDO to all endogeneous variables (components of anti-Semitism, rejection of responsibility for Jews and anti-Zionism) were not significant.

we believe that anti-Semitic attitudes of young Germans should be seen as part of general hostility towards foreigners. The work of Bergmann and Erb (1991), Lederer and Kindervater (1995), and Heitmeyer (2003) supported this interpretation. Lederer and Kindervater (1995) found that a person who rejects Jews, also rejects foreigners, and vice versa. Heitmeyer (2003) spoke, therefore about anti-Semitism as a part of "group-related misanthropy" (p. 15). This term describes a general syndrome of prejudices, which includes racism, xenophobia, Islamophobia, sexism, and anti-Semitism.

Furthermore, manifest anti-Semitic attitudes are anchored in an authoritarian, violence-supporting, traditional, and politically right-orientated value system, as well as in the approval of historic National Socialism. When teenagers in Germany make such anti-Semitic statements today, they do this perhaps because they do not know how to solve their personal problems in a modern, multi-cultural society (see also Farnen & Meloen, 2000). Therefore, we believe that the latency of anti-Semitism and the rejection of responsibility towards Jews are parts of a common attitude among most young people, and provide a picture of reactions to everyday culture in Germany.

The second study also provides clear empirical evidence of the ability of the extended model to describe anti-Semitic attitudes, with the addition of two further components (exaggerated Israel criticism and anti-Zionism). However, the structural differentiation of manifest and latent anti-Semitism could not be demonstrated in this study. Persons with manifest anti-Semitic attitudes presumably tend to find Jews disagreeable, avoiding contact with them and practicing subtle forms of discrimination against them. This conflicts, however, with the idea that latent anti-Semitic persons do not hold manifest attitudes in every case. Another explanation could be a possible overlap of contents of the manifest and latent constructs. The small number of people who exclusively demonstrate latent anti-Semitic attitudes may also evoke this effect. The most powerful explanation is probably provided by the following interpretation, however: Latent anti-Semitic persons respond more to act in a socially desirable fashion. Anti-Semitic prejudices are less pronounced in these persons than in manifest anti-Semitic individuals and they therefore have no need for a substitute form of communication. In addition, the latent attitude is not an expression of a politically marginalized position. A further result of this study indicates that anti-Semites reject German responsibility towards Jews. It is possible that the acceptance of responsibility by anti-Semites would result in a state of cognitive dissonance for them. In a similar way, such an attitude might operate in conjunction with a general national sentiment, of opposition to the acceptance of guilt and responsibility.

Furthermore, the criticism of Israel and anti-Zionism can possibly be taken as confirmation of anti-Semitic attitudes, as it may serve as a form of substitutional communication in public if there are strong social sanctions against the direct communication of one's own prejudices. This is conjecture, however, as it still has to be demonstrated that there is no distinction made between the politics of the state of Israel and Jews in general. This issue, therefore, requires further investigation.

The results of the second study also demonstrate that anti-Semitism and its modern forms or derivations are more strongly influenced by authoritarianism than by SDO. The influence of RWA on manifest and latent anti-Semitic attitudes is particularly positive. Furthermore, RWA is able to predict the rejection of responsibility towards Jews, as well as, to a more moderate degree, the intense criticism of Israel. These results verify the hypothesis that the old and manifest forms of anti-Semitic attitudes can be almost completely explained by RWA. The remarkable predictive qualities of SDO with regards to ethnocentrism and xenophobia raise the question of why this construct has no explanatory power with regards to anti-Semitic attitudes. Perhaps, people with a high SDO do not perceive the Jewish minority and the Israeli-Palestinian conflict as a threat to the status and power of the ingroup.

Turner and Reynolds (2003) offered another, general argument. They argued that social dominance theory is flawed by conceptual inconsistencies and has been disconfirmed empirically in relation to its key hypothesis of group-based hierarchy formation. The reaction of subordinate groups to the social hierarchy could be better explained by social identity theory.

The zero-correlations between the RWA, SDO, and political orientations on the one side, and the anti-Semitic attitudes and their derivations on the other, suggests the necessity of identifying further unknown variables to explain the syndrome of anti-Jewish, anti-Israeli, and anti-Zionist prejudice.

This result, in combination with the positive correlation between RWA and SDO, and the critique of SDT, emphasizes the importance of further investigations.

Another factor, which requires explanation, is the moderate, but significant influence of political orientation on the dimension of exaggerated Israel criticism. The results show that participants who are politically orientated towards the left are particularly motivated to voice their anti-Zionist attitudes. Two interpretations are possible. First, exaggerated Israel criticism amongst left-orientated Germans is also a sign of latent anti-Jewish prejudices. But, the low scores of the left-orientated Germans on the dimensions of manifest and latent anti-Semitism and rejection of responsibility for Jews speak against this interpretation. Right-orientated participants show significantly higher values on these dimensions than left-orientated participants. Second, the exaggerated Israel criticism amongst left-orientated Germans is independent of anti-Semitism; as although modern German anti-Semitic prejudices can take the form of exaggerated Israel criticism, there is also an exaggerated Israel criticism, which is not based on anti-Semitism.

We propose a similar relation between anti-Zionism and anti-Semitism: Anti-Semitism can be expressed in anti-Semitic statements but there is also anti-Zionism without anti-Semitism. In this context, Klug (2003) pointed to the difficulties in assessing the extent to which the new wave of hostility towards Jews, radiating out from the Middle East, is anti-Semitic or not (see also EUMC, 2004, p. 231).

CONCLUSION AND FINAL REMARKS

The basic concern of both studies was the investigation of the structure of anti-Semitic attitudes, their derivations, and their potential influencing factors. The two studies demonstrate that our heuristic models of anti-Semitic attitudes could be useful tools to improve the understanding of the relation between an old-fashioned stereotype and its newer manifestations.

From our data and the results of other analyses, we can state that the post-fascistic anti-Semitism in Germany possesses the following characteristic: It is anti-Semitism devoid of ideology, which did not, however, disappear. Neither did it develop into a simple prejudice. It is related to xenophobia and prejudices towards foreigners in general. It is a latent anti-Semitism, meaning that people do not offer their negative attitudes about Jews publicly. It is a private prejudice whose open expression is taboo. However, political groups can exploit these private prejudices. Anti-Semitic attitudes are related to prejudice and stereotypes concerning Israel. However, further investigations are necessary to demonstrate the causal relations between anti-Semitism, anti-Zionism, and anti-Israeli expressions. Following the report on "Manifestations of anti-Semitism in the EU 2002–2003" we maintain that in cases in which Israel is seen as being representative of "the Jew, anti-Israeli or anti-Zionist attitudes are anti-Semitic" (EUMC, 2004, p. 240). If this is the case, the Israel–Palestinian conflict seems to stand as a substitute for the old anti-Semitism.

Finally, we can conclude that the topic of anti-Semitism in Germany is inseparably connected with German identity. This counts for the present as well as for the future. The reconciliation between Germans and Jews will basically depend on how the next generations deal with the consequences of their shared history. In addition, the next generation of research has to allow for the theoretical, empirical, and methodical challenges of this constantly changing subject. The main topics of reconciliation, inner peace, coming to terms with a negative history, and guilt will remain as constants within anti-Semitism research.

ACKNOWLEDGMENTS

These studies were conducted as part of a research project funded by the Volkswagenstiftung or as part of an extensive student research project.

We are very grateful to Friedrich Funke, Jens Jirschitzka, Sebastian Petzold, Miriam Rieck, and Silke Zachariae for their assistance, and Richard Wagner, Jonathan Ipser, Kitty Dumont, and the anonymous reviewers for their helpful comments and suggestions on an earlier draft.

BIOGRAPHICAL NOTES

Wolfgang Frindte, born 1951, studied psychology; PhD in psychology, Friedrich Schiller University (FSU), Jena, 1981; research associate at the Saxony Academy of Sciences, 1977–1986; habilitation, *venia legendi* (the right to read) in psychology at FSU, 1987; Department of Education of the Teachers College Erfurt/Mühlhausen 1986–1987; Full Professor of Social Psychology, Department of Psychology, FSU, 1987–1996; since 1996 Professor of Communication Psychology, FSU. His research interests lie in the field of political psychology, intercultural communication and media-based communication.

Susan Wettig, born 1976, studied psychology at the Friedrich Schiller University (FSU), Jena, 1995–2000; research associate, Communication Psychology Unit, FSU, 2001–2004; member of the Independent Research Group at the Faculty of Educational Science, University of Erfurt, since 2004. Her research interests lie in the field of stereotypes, prejudices, social group phenomena, and applied social psychology.

Dorit Wammetsberger, born 1975, studied psychology at Friedrich Schiller University (FSU), Jena, Diploma (MA) 2000; since 2001 research associate, Communication Psychology Unit, FSU. Her research interests focus on political psychology, especially anti-Semitism and national identity.

REFERENCES

Adorno, T. W., Frenkel-Brunswik, E., Levinson, D. J., & Sanford, R. N. (1950). *The authoritarian personality.* New York: Harper's.

Allport, G. W. (1935). Attitudes. In C. Murchinson (Ed.), *Handbook of Social Psychology* (pp. 798–884). Worcester, MA: Clark University Press.

Altemeyer, B. (1988). *Enemies of freedom: Understanding ring-wing-authoritarism.* San Francisco: Jossey Bass.

Altemeyer, B. (1996). *The authoritarian specter.* Cambridge, MA.: Harvard University Press.

Altemeyer, B. (1998). The other "authoritarian personality." *Advances in Experimental Social Psychology, 30,* 47–92.

Arbuckle, J. L., & Wothke, W. (1999). *AMOS 4.0 users' guide.* Chicago: Smallwaters Corp.

Bergmann, W., & Erb, R. (1991). *Antisemitismus in der Bundesrepublik Deutschland. Ergebnisse der empirischen Forschung von 1946–1989 [Anti-Semitism in the Federal Republic of Germany. Results of the empirical research 1946–1989].* Opladen, Germany: Leske+Budrich.

Bergmann, W., & Erb, R. (1997). *Anti-Semitism in Germany: The post-Nazi epoch since 1945.* New Brunswick, NJ: Transaction.

Bergmann, W., & Erb, R. (2000). Antisemitismus in der Bundesrepublik Deutschland 1996 [Anti-Semitism in the Federal Republic of Germany 1996]. In R. Alba, P. Schmidt, & M. Wasmer (Eds.), *Deutsche und Auslaender: Freunde, Fremde oder Feinde* (pp. 401–438). Opladen, Germany: Westdeutscher Verlag.

Broder, H. (1986). *Der ewige Antisemit. Über Sinn und Funktion eines beständigen Gefühls* [*The eternal anti-Semite. About meaning and function of a persistant prejudice*]. Frankfurt am Main, Germany: Fischer Verlag.

Dahmer, H. (1993). Antisemitismus und xenophobie [Anti-Semitism and xenophobia]. In H.-U. Otto & R. Merten (Eds.), *Rechtsradikale gewalt im vereinigten Deutschland. Jugend im gesellschaftlichen umbruch* (pp 80–87). Opladen, Germany: Leske+Budrich.

Duckitt, J. (1992). Psychology and prejudice. A historical analysis and integrative framework. *American Psychologist, 47*(10), 1182–1193.

Duckitt, J., Wagner, C., du Plessis, I., & Birum, I. (2002). The psychological bases of ideology and prejudice: Testing a dual process model. *Journal of Personality & Social Psychology, 83,* 75–93.

Duncan, L. E., Peterson, B. E., & Winter, D. G. (1997). Authoritarianism and gender roles: Toward a psychological analysis of hegemonic relationships. *Personality and Social Psychology Bulletin, 23,* 41–49.

Duriez, B., & van Hiel, A. (2002). The march of modern fascism. A comparison of social dominance orientation and authoritarianism. *Personality & Individual Differences, 32,* 1199–1213.

Eisinga, R., Konig, R., & Scheepers, P. (1995). Orthodox religious beliefs and anti-Semitism: A replication of Glock and Stark in the Netherlands. *Journal for Scientific Study of Religion, 34*(2), 214–223.

Enyedi, Z. (1999). Erklärungsmodelle des Antisemitismus [Models of explanation for anti-Semitism]. In W. Benz (Ed.), *Jahrbuch für Antisemitismusforschung 8* (pp. 228–247). Frankfurt am Main, New York: Campus Verlag.

EUMC—European Monitoring Centre on Racism and Xenophobia. (2004). *Report "Manifestations of anti-Semitism in the EU 2002–2003".* Retrieved April 20, 2004, from http://eumc.eu.int/eumc/index.php?fuseaction=content.dsp_cat_content&catid=1

Eurobarometer. (2003). *Flash Eurobarometer 151 "Iraq and peace in the world".* Retrieved April 15, 2003, from http://europa.eu.int/comm/public_opnion/flash/fl151_iraq_full_report.pdf.

Farnen, R. F., & Meloen, J. D. (2000). *Democracy, authoritarianism and education: A cross-national empirical survey.* Basingstoke, London: Macmillan.

Freedland, J. (2003). Is anti-Zionism anti-Semitism? In P. Iganski & B. Kosmin (Eds.), *A new anti-Semitism? Debating Judeophobia in 21st Century Britain* (pp. 119–126). London: Profile.

Frindte, W., Funke, F., & Jacob, S. (1997). Autoritarismus, Wertorientierungen und jugendkulturelle Identifikation—eine sozialpsychologische Analyse deutscher Jugendlicher [Authoritarianism, value orientations, and adolescents' identification patterns: A social psychology analysis of German adolescents]. *Gruppendynamik, 28*(3), 273–289.

Frindte, W., Funke, F., & Jacob, S. (1999). Neu-alte Mythen über Juden: Ein Forschungsbericht [Recent and old myths about Jews. A research report]. In R. Dollase, T. Kliche, & H. Moser (Eds.), *Politische Psychologie der Fremdenfeindlichkeit. Opfer, Täter, Mittäter* (pp. 119–130). Weinheim, Germany: Juventa.

Frindte, W., Funke, F., Jacob, S., & Carmil, D. (1999). *Jugendliche einstellungen gegenüber "Fremden"—Ein sozialpsychologischer Vergleich zwischen deutschen und israelischen Jugendlichen* [*Research report: Adolescent attitudes towards "strangers"—A social psychological comparison between German and Israeli adolescents*]. Unpublished research report, Friedrich-Schiller-Universität Jena, Germany.

Frindte, W., Wammetsberger, D., & Wettig, S. (2003). Antisemitische Einstellungen Deutscher Jugendlicher [Anti-Semitic attitudes of German adolescents]. In E. H. Witte (Ed.), *Sozialpsychologie Politischer Prozesse: Beiträge des 18. Hamburger Symposiums zur Methodologie der Sozialpsychologie* [Social psychology of political processes: Report from the 18th Hamburger Symposium on the Methodology of Social Psychology] (pp. 34–57). Lengerich, Germany: Pabst.

Funke, F. (2002). *Die dreidimensionale Struktur von Autoritarismus* [The three dimensional structure of authoritarianism]. Unpublished doctoral dissertation, Friedrich-Schiller-Universität Jena, Germany.

Gibson, J. L., & Duch, R. M. (1992). Anti-Semitic attitudes of the mass public: Estimates and explanations based on a survey of the Moscow Oblast. *Public Opinion Quartley, 56*(1), 1–28.

Heaven, P. C. L., & Connors, J. R. (2001). A note on the value correlates of social dominance orientation and right-wing authoritarianism. *Personality & Individual Differences, 31,* 925–930.

Heitmeyer, W. (Ed.) (2003). *Deutsche zustände (Bd. 2)* [German situations (Volume II)]. Frankfurt a.M., Germany: Suhrkamp.

Horkheimer, M., & Adorno, T. W. (1944). *Dialektik der aufklärung [Dialectics of enlightenment].* Frankfurt a. M., Germany: Fischer.

Jöreskog, K. G., Sörbom, D., du Toit, S., & du Toit, M. (1999). *LISREL 8: New statistical features.* Chicago: Scientific Software International.

Kindervater, A. (2004, July). *Authoritarianism and anti-Semitism: A comparison of attitudes in border regions of Germany and Poland.* Paper presented at the Annual Conference of the International Society of Political Psychology, Lund, Sweden.

Klug, B. (2003). The collective Jew: Israel and the new anti-Semitism. *Patterns of Prejudice, 37* (2), 124–137.

Kovács, A. (1999a). Antisemitic prejudices in contemporary Hungary. In The Vidal Sassoon International Center for the study of Antisemitism (Eds.), *Analyses of current trends in Antisemitism* (pp. 48–58). Jerusalem, Israel: Hebrew University of Jerusalem.

Kovács, A. (1999b). Antisemitismus im heutigen Ungarn—Ein Forschungsbericht [Anti-Semitism in contemporary Hungary—A research report]. In W. Benz (Ed.), *Jahrbuch für Antisemitismusforschung 8* (pp. 195–227). Frankfurt am Main, New York: Campus Verlag.

Lederer, G., & Kindervater, A. (1995). Wandel des autoritarismus bei Jugendlichen in Österreich [Changing authoritarianism of young people in Austria]. In G. Lederer & P. Schmidt (Eds.), *Autoritarismus und gesellschaft* [Authoritarianism and society] (pp. 136–166). Opladen, Germany: Leske+Budrich.

Lederer, G., & Schmidt, P. (1995). Autoritarismus und gesellschaft [Authoritarianism and society]. Opladen, Germany: Leske+Budrich.

Levin, S., Federico, C. M., Sidanius, J., & Rabinowitz, J. L. (2002). Social dominance orientation and intergroup bias: The legitimation of favoritism for high-status groups. *Personality and Social Psychology Bulletin, 28,* 144–157.

Lippa, R., & Arad, S. (1999). Gender, personality, and prejudice: The display of authoritarianism and social dominance in interviews with college men and women. *Journal of Research in Personality, 33,* 463–493.

Marin, B. (1980). A post-Holocaust "anti-Semitism without anti-Semites"? Austria as a case in point. *Political Psychology, 2*(2), 57–74.

Martire, G., & Clark, R. (1982). *Anti-Semitism in the United States. A study of prejudice in the 1980s.* New York: Praeger.

McFarland, S., Ageyev, V., & Abalakina, M. (1993). The authoritarian personality in the United States and the former Soviet Union: Comparative studies. In W. F. Stone, G. Lederer, & R. Christie (Eds.), *Strength and weakness. The authoritarian personality today* (pp. 199–225). New York: Springer.

Meloen, J. (1991). The fortieth anniversary of "The Authoritarian Personality". *Politics and the Individual, 1*(1), 119–127.

Oesterreich, D. (1996). *Flucht in die sicherheit—Zur Theorie des Autoritarismus und der Autoritären Reaktion* [Escape into the security—The theory of authoritarianism and the authoritarian reaction]. Opladen, Germany: Leske+Budrich.

Pettigrew, T. F., & Meertens, R. W. (1995). Subtle and blatant prejudice in western Europe. *European Journal of Social Psychology, 25,* 57–75.

Petzold, S. (2004). *Antisemitische Einstellungen in Deutschland—Eine Explorationsstudie [Anti-Semitic attitudes in Germany—An explorative study].* Unpublished dissertation, Friedrich-Schiller-Universität Jena, Germany.

Pratto, F., Sidanius, J., Stallworth, M., & Malle, B. F. (2001). Social dominance orientation: A personality variable predicting social and political attitudes. In M. A. Hogg & D. Abrams (Eds.), *Intergroup relations. Essential readings* (pp. 31–128). Philadelphia: Psychology Press.

Raden, D. (1993). Relationships between anti-Semitism and authoritarian attitudes in a national survey. *Psychological Reports, 73,* 209–210.

Raden, D. (1999). Is anti-Semitism currently part of an authoritarian attitude syndrome? *Political Psychology, 20,* 323–343.

Rippl, S., Seipel, C., & Kindervater, A. (2000). *Autoritarismus. Kontroversen und ansätze der aktuellen autoritarismusforschung.* [Authoritarianism. Controversies and approaches of current research]. Opladen, Germany: Leske + Budrich.

Selznick, G., & Steinberg, S. (1969). *The tenacy of prejudice. Antisemitism in contemporary America.* New York: Harper & Row.

Sidanius, J., & Pratto, F. (1993). The inevitability of oppression and the dynamics of social dominance. In P. M. Sniderman & P. E. Tetlock (Eds.), *Prejudice, politics, and the American dilemma* (pp. 173–211). Palo Alto, CA: Stanford University Press.

Sidanius, J., & Pratto, F. (1999). *Social dominance: An intergroup theory of social hierarchy and oppression.* Cambridge, UK: Cambridge University Press.

Sidanius, J., Pratto, F., & Bobo, L. (1994). Social dominance orientation and the political psychology of gender: A case of invariance? *Journal of Personality & Social Psychology, 67,* 998–1011.

Six, B., Wolfradt, U., & Zick, A. (2001). Autoritarismus und Soziale Dominanzorientierung als generalisierte Einstellungen [Authoritarianism and social dominance orientation as generalized attitudes]. *Zeitschrift für Politische Psychologie, 9,* 23–40.

Smith, A. G., & Winter, D. G. (2002). Right-wing authoritarianism, party identification, and attitudes toward feminism in student evaluations of the Clinton-Lewinsky story. *Political Psychology, 23,* 355–383.

Smith, T. W. (1993). The polls—A review. Actual trends or measurement artifacts? A review of three studies of anti-Semitism. *Public Option Quarterly, 57,* 380–393.

Spiegel, P. (2002). TV-Interview with broadcast station "Phoenix." Broadcasted June 17, 2002.

Stone, W. F., Lederer, G., & Christie, R. (1993). *Strength and weakness. The authoritarian personality today.* New York: Springer.

Sturzbecher, D., & Freytag, R. (2000). *Antisemitismus unter Jugendlichen* [Anti-Semitism among adolescents]. Göttingen, Germany: Hogrefe.

Turner, J. C., & Reynolds, K. J. (2003). Why social dominance theory has been falsified. *British Journal of Social Psychology, 42,* 199–206.

Van Hiel, A., & Mervielde, I. (2002). Explaining conservative beliefs and political preferences: A comparison of social dominance orientation and authoritarianism. *Journal of Applied Social Psychology, 32,* 965–976.

Wagner, U., van Dick, R., & Zick, A. (2001). Sozialpsychologische Analysen und Erklärungen von Fremdenfeindlichkeit in Deutschland [Social psychological analysis and explanations of xenophobia in Germany]. *Zeitschrift fuer Sozialpsychologie, 32,* 59–79.

Weiss, H. (1999). On the present-day significance of the concept of the "authoritarian personality". In Z. Enyedy & F. Erös (Eds.), *Authoritarianism and prejudice. Central European perspectives* (pp. 29–53). Budapest, Hungary: Osiris.

Whitley, B. E. J. (1999). Right-wing authoritarianism, social dominance orientation, and prejudice. *Journal of Personality & Social Psychology, 77,* 126–134.

Wittenberg, R., & Schmidt, M. (2003). Antisemitische einstellungen in Deutschland in den Jahren 1994 und 2002 [Anti-Semitic attitudes in Germany in 1994 and 2002] (Working paper 2003–4). Erlangen-Nuernberg, Germany: Friedrich-Alexander-University.

Zachariae, S. (2003). *Autoritarismus und Soziale Dominanzorientierung vor dem Hintergrund von Persönlichkeit und Fremdenfeindlichen Einstellungen [Authoritarianism and social dominance orientation against the background of personality and xenophobic attitudes].* Unpublished dissertation, Friedrich-Schiller-Universität Jena, Germany.

APPENDIX

Examples for indicators of all concepts measured are listed in the following. Response format was a five-point scale, on which respondents indicated how much they agreed or disagreed to the statements presented (e.g., 1 = *agree not at all* to 5 = *agree very much*). A minus sign in brackets following an item indicates that it has been reversed. All items are listed in the original German version, as in the questionnaire used. For a better understanding, all listed items are translated, but please note there are no verified English versions in every case. Hence, merely the headlines of the subscales are translated in English to ensure better orientation. For German and English versions of Study 1 see Frindte, Funke, & Jacob, 1999 and Frindte, Funke, Jacob, & Carmil, 1999.

STUDY 1: Anti-Semitism Scale
(for a German version see also Bergmann & Erb, 1991)

Subscale manifest anti-Semitism

asma1   Es wäre besser für Deutschland, keine Juden im Land zu haben.
        [It's better for Germany to have no Jews at all.]

asma2   In Deutschland haben die Juden zuviel Einfluss.
        [The Jews in Germany have too much influence.]

asma3   Juden haben auf der Welt zuviel Einfluss.
        [The Jews have too much influence over the world.]

asma4   Ich gehöre zu denen. Die keine Juden mögen.
        [I don't like Jews.]

asma5   Juden sollten keine höheren Positionen im Staate innehaben.
        [The Jews should not hold higher positions in the government.]

asma6   Mit Juden sollte man keine Geschäfte machen.
        [One should avoid having business dealings with Jews.]

Subscale rejection of responsibility for Jews

aresp1   Das deutsche Volk hat eine besondere Verantwortung gegenüber den Juden.
  [The German people must take a special responsibility for the Jews.]

asresp2   Als heute lebender Jugendlicher muss man nicht mehr über die Schuld der Deutschen gegenüber den Juden nachdenken.
  [As a young person in Germany, I don't have to be responsible for the Jews.]

asresp3   Jahrzehnte nach Kriegsende sollten wir nicht mehr soviel über die Judenverfolgung reden, sondern endlich einen Schlussstrich unter die Vergangenheit ziehen.
  [Decades after the end of the war, we should not talk so much about the Holocaust. We should close the discussions about the past.]

Subscale latent anti-Semitism

aslat1   Ich glaube, dass sich viele nicht trauen, ihre wirkliche Meinung über Juden zu sagen.
  [I think that many people do not reveal their true opinion about Jews.]

aslat2   Mir ist das ganze Thema "Juden" irgendwie unangenehm.
  [The subject "Jew" is an unpleasant thing for me.]

aslat3   Was ich über Juden denke, sage ich nicht jedem.
  [I do not talk to just anyone about Jews.]

Attitudes toward foreigners (Xenophobia)

af5   Die Ausländer sollen ihre Kultur in ihrem Land pflegen. Hier in diesem Land sollen sie sich anpassen.
  [The foreigners, once in Germany, have to adjust to the German culture.]

af8   In Deutschland sollten nur Deutsche leben.
  [It is desirable that only Germans live in Germany.]

af39   Deutsche sollten keine Ausländer heiraten.
  [Germans should not marry Non-Germans.]

af15   Ausländer provozieren durch ihr Verhalten selbst die Ausländerfeindlichkeit.
  [The foreigners arouse hostility by their very behavior.]

af23   Die meisten Politiker in Deutschland sorgen sich zu sehr um die Ausländer und nicht um Otto-Normalverbraucher.
  [Most politicians worry too much about the foreigners and don't care for the regular citizen.]

af32   Die Ausländer haben Jobs, die eigentlich wir Deutschen haben sollten.
  [The foreigners take the jobs of the Germans.]

af38   Ausländer in Deutschland sollten sich nicht hindrängen, wo sie nicht gemocht werden.
  [Foreigners should not push themselves to places where they don't belong.]

Acceptance of Violence

acvio1   Es ist völlig normal, wenn Männer sich im körperlichen Kampf mit anderen selbst beweisen wollen.
  [It is perfectly OK . for men to prove themselves by fighting.]

acvio2   Ich bin gegen jede Form von Gewalt. (-)
  [I am against any kind of violence.]

acvio6   Mädchen stiften Jungen manchmal zu einer Schlägerei an.
  [Sometimes boys are tempted into a fight by girls.]

acvio8	Ich würde selbst nie körperliche Gewalt anwenden. Aber ich finde es gut, wenn es Leute gibt, die auf diese Weise für Ordnung sorgen.
	[I will never use force myself, but I accept the use of force by others to achieve order.]
acvio12	Im Zusammenleben von Menschen wird letztlich alles über Gewalt geregelt.
	[Eventually everything is dealt with force.]
acvio15	Gewaltaktionen sind zur Lösung von Konflikten nicht geeignet. (-)
	[Violence is not an efficient measure in solving conflicts.]
acvio17	Zur Durchsetzung politischer Interessen ist Gewalt gerechtfertigt.
	[It is justified to use force for political purposes.]
acvio21	Um persönliche Interessen durchzusetzen, sollte keine Gewalt angewendet werden. (-)
	[One should not use force to achieve personal interests.]
acvio22	Gewalt ist etwas völlig Normales, weil sie überall vorkommt.
	[Violence is normal since it happens all the time all over the world.]

Readiness for violence

vio4	Ich wäre bereit, meine persönlichen Konflikte auch mit Gewalt zu lösen.
	[I am ready to use violence to solve my problems.]
vio7	Um auf Probleme aufmerksam zu machen, würde ich auch Gewalt anwenden.
	[I am ready to use violence in order to attract attention to my problems.]
vio10	Manchmal macht es mir Spaб, mich an gewalttätigen Aktionen zu beteiligen.
	[Sometimes it's fun to fight.]
vio13	Zur Durchsetzung politischer Interessen würde ich mich auch an gewalttätigen Demonstrationen beteiligen.
	[I am ready to participate in violent demonstrations to achieve political goals.]
vio11	Ich würde Gewalt gegen Ausländer ausüben.
	[I would use force against immigrants.]

Right-wing authoritarianism scale (Altemeyer, 1988, Short version)

rwa12	Gehorsam und Achtung vor der Autorität sind die wichtigsten Tugenden, die Kinder lernen sollten.
	[One of the most important properties children should learn is discipline and respect to authority.]
rwa26	Die wahren Schlüssel zum "guten Leben" sind Gehorsam, Disziplin und Prinzipienfestigkeit.
	[The key to the good life is obedience, discipline, and accepted behavior.]
rwa3	Man tut immer besser daran, dem Urteil der Zuständigen in Regierung und Kirche zu trauen, als auf die lauten Unruhestifter in unserer Gesellschaft zu hören, die nur Zweifel in den Köpfen der Menschen säen wollen.
	[It is always better to trust the authorities of government or religion than those who try to doubt.]

Approval of the repetition of national-socialism.

Würden Sie eine Wiederholung des Nationalsozialismus für gut heiben?

[Would you agree to a repetition of national socialism?]

Political orientation

Würden Sie sich eher als links oder rechts bezeichnen?

[Would you classify your own political orientation more left or more right?]

Subscale manifest and latent anti-Semitism.

asma3   Mit Juden sollte man keine Geschäfte machen.
[One should avoid having business dealings with Jews.]

asma7   Ich gehöre zu denen, die keine Juden mögen.
[I don't like Jews.]

asma8   Es wäre besser für Deutschland, keine Juden im Land zu haben.
[It's better for Germany to have no Jews at all]

asma9   Juden sollten keine höheren Positionen im Staate innehaben.
[The Jews should not hold higher positions in the government.]

asma10   In Deutschland haben die Juden zuviel Einfluss.
[The Jews in Germany have too much influence.]

aslat1   Ehen zwischen Juden und Nicht-Juden sollten besser vermieden werden.
[Marriages between Jews and non-Jews should be avoided.]

aslat2   Es ist besser, mit Juden nicht zu tun zu haben.
[One should not interact with Jews.]

aslat7   Die hier lebenden Juden sollten sich nicht dort hineindrängen, wo man sie nicht haben will.
[Jews living here should not push themselves where they are not wanted.]

aslat8   Mir ist das ganze Thema Juden irgendwie unangenehm.
[The subject "Jew" is an unpleasant thing for me.]

aslat11   Die Juden erziehen ihre Kinder zu anderen Werten und Fähigkeiten, als hier in der Bundesrepublik gebraucht werden, um erfolgreich zu sein.
[Jews teach their children values and skills different from those required to be successful in Germany.]

Subscale rejection of responsibility for Jews

asver1   Viele Juden versuchen heute, aus der Vergangenheit einen Vorteil zu ziehen.
[Many Jews try to take advantage of their own history.]

asver4   Jahrzehnte nach Kriegsende sollten wir nicht mehr so viel über die Judenverfolgung reden, sondern endlich einen Schlussstrich unter die Vergangenheit ziehen.
[Decades after the end of the war, we should not talk so much about the Holocaust. We should close the discussions about the past.]

asver5   Man sollte endlich mit dem Gerede über unsere Schuld gegenüber den Juden Schluss machen.
[One should finally stop the discussion about our guilt towards the Jews.]

asver6   Das deutsche Volk hat eine besondere Verantwortung gegenüber den Juden. (-)
[The German people must take a special responsibility for the Jews.]

Subscale exaggerated anti-Israeli attitudes (criticism on Israel)

ikrit3   Israel ist allein schuldig an der Entstehung und Aufrechterhaltung der Konflikte im Nahen Osten.
[Israel is solely responsible for the development and maintenance of the conflicts in the Middle East.]

ikrit5   Israel ist ein Staat, der über Leichen geht.
[Israel is a state that stops at nothing.]

ikrit9   Die Israelis sind Besatzer und haben in den Palästinensergebieten nichts zu suchen.

[Israelis are illegitimate occupiers of the Palestinian areas.]

ikrit11   Was die Israelis den Palästinensern antun, ähnelt dem, was die Nazis den Juden angetan haben.

[The way Israelis deal with Palestinians is similar to what Nazi Germany did to the Jews.]

Subscale anti-Zionism

azio1   Die Gründung des israelischen Staates war ein Fehler.

[The foundation of the state Israel was a mistake.]

azio3   Es wäre besser, wenn die Juden den Nahen Osten verlassen würden.

[It would be better if the Jews would leave the Middle East.]

Right-wing authoritarianism scale (RWA3D; for the full German version see Funke, 2002)

rwa6s   Gehorsam und Achtung vor der Autorität sind die wichtigsten Tugenden, die Kinder lernen sollten.

[One of the most important properties children should learn is discipline and respect to authority.]

rwa12s   Die wahren Schlüssel zum guten Leben sind Gehorsam, Disziplin und Tugend.

[The key to the good life is obedience, discipline, and accepted behaviour.]

Social dominance orientation scale (SDO; for the full English version see Sidanius & Pratto, 1999; for a German version see Zachariae, 2003)

sdo2   Soziale Gleichheit sollte zunehmen. (-)

[Increased social equality]

sdo11   Wir würden weniger Probleme haben, wenn wir Menschen gleicher behandeln würden. (-)

[If people were treated more equally, we would have fewer problems in this country.]

sdo13   Einige Menschen sind anderen gegenüber einfach unterlegen.

[Some people are just inferior to others.]

Political orientation

Würden Sie sich eher als links oder rechts bezeichnen?

[Would you classify your own political orientation more left or more right?]

PEACE AND CONFLICT: JOURNAL OF PEACE PSYCHOLOGY, *11*(3), 267–292

The Cognitive Representation of Human Rights: Knowledge, Importance, and Commitment

Jost Stellmacher and Gert Sommer
University of Marburg

Elmar Brähler
University of Leipzig

The Universal Declaration of Human Rights (United Nations, 2002) is an important ethical framework for political actions. In this declaration, and in the subsequent International Covenants (United Nations, 2002), 2 major classes of human rights are distinguished, one consisting of civil and political rights, and the other consisting of economic, social, and cultural rights. The Universal Declaration itself and the UN Decade for Human Rights Education emphasize the relevance of an adequate knowledge about human rights in the population. Accordingly, this article represents the results of 2 representative studies on human rights in Germany. The major results of these studies are that knowledge about human rights and about human rights documents is quite low. Also, economic, social, and cultural rights are less known, and are evaluated as less important, than civil and political rights. Thus, the idea of the indivisibility of human rights is not realized. Relating to the commitment to human rights, about 1% of the population might be labeled as core activists. However, large interindividual differences concerning the commitment to human rights were observed. These differences can be explained in part by knowledge about human rights and by the importance of human rights. Right-wing authoritarianism and social dominance orientation show only inconsistent results.

Additionally, some relevant differences between East Germans and West Germans were found. East Germans showed greater knowledge about, and somewhat higher appreciation of economic human rights, especially concerning the right to work. Altogether, the results emphasize the importance of a more extensive human rights education.

Correspondence should be sent to Gert Sommer, Department of Psychology, University of Marburg, Gutenbergstr. 18, 35037 Marburg, Germany. E-mail: sommerg@staff.uni-marburg.de

> Human rights are the foundation of human existence and coexistence. They are universal, indivisible, and interdependent. And they lie at the heart of everything the United Nations aspires to achieve in its global mission of peace and development. (Kofi Annan, UN Secretary General quoted in United Nations, 2002, p. XIII)

The Universal Declaration of Human Rights (UDHR), which was adopted by the General Assembly of the United Nations in 1948 (United Nations [UN], 1995), is the main reference document for human rights. This declaration consists of 30 articles, which comprise more than 100 specific rights. The preamble of the UDHR emphasizes that these rights are inalienable, that they are a common standard of achievement for all peoples and all nations, that every individual and every organ of society shall strive to promote respect for these rights, and that national and international measures are to be taken to secure their universal recognition.

Two "generations" of human rights are distinguished in the UDHR, as well as in the two subsequent International Covenants on Human Rights of 1966 (International Covenant on Economic, Social and Cultural Rights; International Covenant on Civil and Political Rights; see UN, 2002). The first generation consists of civil and political human rights (which we abbreviate in the following text as *civil* human rights): for example, the right to life; the prohibition of torture or cruel, inhuman, or degrading treatment; the right to freedom of thought; of opinion and expression; and the right to political asylum. The second generation is made up of economic, social, and cultural human rights (which we abbreviate as *economic* human rights): for example, the right to work and protection against unemployment; the right to rest and leisure; the right to an adequate standard of living, including food, clothing, housing, and medical care; the right to social security; and the right to education. In addition, a third generation of human rights has been discussed for several years, but has not yet been adopted as a human rights document by the UN. This third generation comprises the right of peoples to peace, the right to development, and the right to a healthy environment (UN, 1995).

The UN claims that human rights are universal, that is, they apply to all people. They also have been proclaimed to be indivisible, which stresses the claim that every right of the UDHR and the International Covenants must be acknowledged and realized, and that there should be no division into civil versus economic rights (see UN, 1995).

The UDHR itself demands that people should be given every opportunity to know their human rights. Article 26 of the UDHR states that "education shall be directed … to the strengthening of human rights" (UN, 2002, p. 5). In a very similar way, the preamble of the UDHR asks teaching and education "to promote respect for these rights." Also, both of the International Covenants ask the States "to promote universal respect for … human rights," and every individual "to strive for the promotion and observance of the rights" (UN, 2002, p. 1) recognized in the Covenants. These statements may be transformed into the following three aspects: people should know their rights, they should appreciate human rights, and they should defend them whenever they are violated.

To promote respect for human rights, the UN Educational, Scientific, and Cultural Organization (UNESCO) has repeatedly recommended steps for human rights education, for example, in 1995, with its "Integrated Framework of Action on Education for Peace, Human Rights and Democracy" (UN, 1999). The General Assembly of the UN also dealt with this topic. In 1994, a "Decade for Human Rights Education" (1995—2004) was announced. Furthermore, the declaration on human rights defenders (cf. UN, 2002, 473–478) emphasized that "Everyone has the right ... to promote and to strive for the protection and realization of human rights" (Article 1) and "to know ... and obtain information about all human rights" (Article 6). After half of the decade for human rights education, however, the evaluation by UN Secretary General Kofi Annan was quite disappointing:

> Five years ago, we began the United Nations Decade of Human Rights Education. ... Today, halfway through the Decade, we still have a long way to go. Only a few countries have developed effective national strategies for human rights education. ... The more people know their own rights, and the more they respect those of others, the better the chance that they will live together in peace. Only when people are educated about human rights can we hope to prevent human rights violations, and thus prevent conflict, as well. (Annan, 2000)

Studying the promotion of respect for human rights is, therefore, a relevant topic for psychological research.

Empirical psychological analyses of human rights in Germany have shown at least two essential problems concerning the cognitive representation of human rights. One major problem is that knowledge about human rights is very poor (Sommer, 1999; Sommer & Zinn, 1996). Secondary school students, for instance, were asked to write down all human rights they could recall spontaneously. On average, the students were able to name only two rights. There were similar findings in a study of university students (Neumann, Evers, Sommer, & Stellmacher, 1999). Likewise, in a study of about 1,000 adults from the United States, only 8% could give the correct answer to the question whether there is "an official document that sets forth human rights for everyone worldwide" (Hart Research Associates, 1997). After the UDHR was identified as this document, 63% of the participants admitted that they had never heard of it before. Also, a cross-national study of psychology students in Finland, Germany, Netherlands, Norway, and former Yugoslavia showed similar deficits (Sommer, Stellmacher, & Christ, 2004). The students had only marginal knowledge about human rights.

A second problem concerns the indivisibility of human rights. According to Ostermann and Nicklas (1979), who analyzed the human rights discourse in the Federal Republic of Germany, there is a distinct division between civil and economic rights. A division between civil and economic rights was also found in an analysis of the way the German print media reflected the 40th anniversary of the UDHR in 1988 (Sommer, Everschor, & Walden, 1992). Accordingly, when subjects were asked to recall human rights spontaneously, civil human rights came to mind first. The various economic human rights were hardly represented cognitively at all (Neumann et al., 1999; Sommer, 1999). Likewise, in the previously mentioned U.S. study (Hart Research Associates, 1997), subjects named eight civil rights but only one economic right as "the first thing that comes to mind" in response to the term "human rights." In different German samples, it was also found that subjects, when confronted with a list of various rights, identify civil rights much more readily as human rights than they do economic rights (Sommer & Zinn, 1996). A similar distinction concerning the importance of human rights was found in samples from Germany and other European countries: Civil human rights were regarded as more important than economic human rights (Sommer, 1999; Sommer et al., 2004).

Several other psychological studies have dealt with the cognitive representation of human rights (e.g., Doise, Spini, & Clémence, 1999; Macek, Osecká, & Kostron, 1997; Moghaddam & Vuksanovic, 1990). However, none of these studies asked for knowledge about human rights. Instead, they first presented a list of examples of human rights (e.g., Moghaddam & Vuksanovic, 1990) or the complete wording of all 30 articles of the UDHR (e.g., Doise et al., 1999). Then subjects were asked to give different evaluations. Therefore, in these studies the actual knowledge people have about human rights remains indeterminate.

AIMS OF THESE STUDIES

This article presents the results of two representative studies on human rights in Germany. In these studies, the knowledge about human rights, the importance of human rights, and the commitment to human rights have been assessed. Three major aims can be defined.

1.   In our former research on knowledge about human rights (see Sommer, 1999), subjects were, with only a few exceptions, university students. Therefore, it is not possible to generalize these results to the general population. Therefore, we conducted two representative studies about human rights in Germany (for preliminary results of the first study, see Sommer, Stellmacher, & Brähler, 2003). One purpose of these studies is to examine the Germans' knowledge about human rights, the importance they ascribe to them, and their willingness to plead for them.

2.   The unification of East Germany and West Germany in 1989 made it possible to compare socialization effects of living in very different ideological systems. East Germany was a so-called socialist country, whereas West Germany may be characterized as a democratic and capitalist country. In the study of human rights,

this comparison is of special interest, because human rights have been an important instrument in political discourse and in the development of enemy images (Sommer, 2001). Western countries accused the socialist countries of violating political and civil human rights, for example, freedom of movement, of religion and opinion, and a lack of democratic elections. As a reaction to this, the Eastern countries have emphasized the violation of economical and social rights by the Western countries, especially the right to work and the right to protection against unemployment. Thus, a second aim of this study is to examine if the different ideologies can still be found in the cognitive representation of human rights.

3.   A recent study by Stellmacher, Sommer, and Imbeck (2003) has shown that there are substantial interindividual differences concerning the willingness to plead for human rights. Knowledge about human rights, their importance, right-wing authoritarianism (RWA; see Adorno, Frenkel-Brunswik, Levinson, & Sanford, 1950; Altemeyer, 1996), and social dominance orientations (SDO; Sidanius & Pratto, 1999) were identified as the main variables that explain such interindividual differences. However, the Stellmacher et al. (2003) study used a selective sample of students and nonstudents. A third aim of this study, therefore, was to examine whether the results of Stellmacher et al. (2003) can be replicated with a more representative sample. Besides knowledge about human rights and the importance of human rights, RWA and SDO were included as predictors as well. We predicted that RWA would be negatively related to the commitment to human rights because high-authoritarians are more likely to adhere to the values and norms set by established authorities and to oppose to individual liberties and freedoms as defined in the human rights declarations. *SDO* is defined as a generalized orientation toward group-based social hierarchy (Sidanius & Pratto, 1999). People with a high SDO accept hierarchies and inequalities between social groups more readily than people with a low SDO. However, hierarchies and inequalities between different social groups are incompatible with the concept of the universality of human rights. Thus, we predicted that people obtaining high scores on the social dominance scale would show less commitment to human rights than people obtaining low scores.

METHOD

The First Representative Study of 2002

The first representative study was conducted in April 2002 by the professional opinion research institute, USUMA (Berlin, Germany). The aim of this study was to evaluate the knowledge about human rights, the importance of human rights, and the willingness to plead for human rights. Additionally, RWA and SDO were assessed as possible predictor variables.

Participants.   Two thousand and fifty-one persons from East Germany (N = 1001) and West Germany (N = 1050) took part in this study. The age of the women

(N = 1052) and the men (N = 999) ranged from 14 to 92 years (M = 45.7; SD = 17.6). The study was conducted via face-to-face-interviews.

Questionnaire

Knowledge about human rights.   The knowledge about human rights was assessed with the question "Please name all human rights you know." This question on knowledge was introduced with the information that "national and international politics often refer to human rights." The responses had been transformed into 60 categories by USUMA. Then the authors assigned these categories to the 30 articles of the UDHR. In addition, the categories were also rated as different single human rights, when they referred to different aspects of the same human rights article. For example, the rights to work, to protection against unemployment, to equal pay for equal work, to just remuneration, and the right to form and to join trade unions, are all different rights within one single article (Article 23). Thus, it was possible to calculate a score on the level of single human rights and a score on the level of human rights articles.

Importance of human rights.   The importance of human rights was assessed with the question "How important do you find the realization of this right?" relating to a list of 22 rights. The items presented were the essential contents of nine civil and eight economic human rights, mostly taken from the UDHR. The items were chosen to represent various important aspects of human rights (for economical reasons, we did not list all human rights of the UDHR). In addition, five distracter items were given to prevent an acquiescence response set, which is the tendency to agree. Participants were asked to answer the items on a 5-point rating scale ranging from 1 (*very unimportant*) to 5 (*very important*).

Willingness to plead for human rights.   This variable was assessed with two items. One indicated the willingness to get actively involved in a human rights organization. The other asked for the willingness to donate money to a human rights organization. Both items could be answered on a 4-point rating scale ranging from 1 (*very unwilling*) to 4 (*very willing*). The scale, which combined both items, showed a reliability of α = .74.

RWA and SDO.   RWA was assessed with two items taken from a short German RWA-scale developed by Petzel, Wagner, Nicolai, and van Dick (1997). SDO was assessed with four items taken from a German SDO-scale developed by Stellmacher and Wagner (1999). The items could be answered on a 4-point rating scale ranging from 1 (*totally disagree*) to 4 (*totally agree*). The reliability of the RWA-scale was α = .62 and that of the SDO-scale was α = .73.

The Second Representative Study of 2003

The second representative study was conducted by USUMA in October 2003. This study was realized in cooperation with the German Institute for Human Rights (Deutsches Institut für Menschenrechte—DIMR, Berlin). The aim of this representative study was to complement the first study by assessing some additional human rights variables concerning knowledge, importance, and support. In addition, RWA and SDO were assessed again.

Participants.   Two thousand and seventeen persons from East Germany (N = 361) and West Germany (N = 1656) took part in the study. The different sample sizes reflect the actual size of the population in both parts of Germany. The age of the women (N = 1042) and the men (N = 974) ranged between 14 and 93 years (*M* = 45.7; *SD* = 18.1). The study was conducted via telephone interviews.

Questionnaire

Knowledge about human rights declarations.   Participants were asked, "As far as you know, is there an official document that sets forth human rights for everyone worldwide?" If the answer was "yes," subjects were asked to tell, if possible, the name of this document or these documents.

Knowledge about human rights.   Participants were presented with a list of 20 rights and asked, "How certain are you that the listed right is a human right?" Responses could be given on a 5-point rating scale ranging from 1 (*certainly not*) to 5 (*certainly yes*). The items presented were the essential, mostly verbatim, contents of ten civil and eight economic human rights taken from the UDHR. Additionally, two other "rights" were presented as distracter items to prevent an acquiescence response set.

Importance of human rights.   In this study, the importance of human rights was assessed with one item, "How important do you find the realization of human rights for every human being worldwide?" Responses were given on a 5-point rating scale ranging from 1 (*very unimportant*) to 5 (*very important*).

Commitment to human rights.   The active support of human rights in the last 5 years was assessed with four items dealing with (a) donating money to a human rights organization, (b) signing petitions to protest against human rights violations, (c) taking part in demonstrations or picketing to protest against human rights violations, and (d) being actively involved in a human rights organization. The first three items could be answered on a 4-point rating scale ranging from 1 (*never*) to 4 (*often*). The "involvement" item could be answered with "yes" or "no." Because of the low correlations between these items, no combined scale could be generated.

RWA and SDO.   Because of the reliability problems of the RWA and SDO scales in the 2002 study, we decided to use other scales that have been successful in previous representative German studies (Heitmeyer, 2002). RWA was assessed with four items and SDO with three items. The items could be answered on a 4-point rating scale ranging from 1 (*totally disagree*) to 4 (*totally agree*). For the RWA scale, coefficient $\alpha = .69$; for the SDO scale $\alpha = .58$.

RESULTS

Representative Results for Germany

To calculate results in a way that is representative of the German population, we used weights for each participant that were allocated by USUMA. These weights correct deviations of specific sample characteristics from their actual distribution in the German population, especially with respect to the gender, age, and size of population in each federal state.

Knowledge About Human Rights Declarations

In response to the question of whether there is a document that defines human rights for every human being worldwide, 49.8% of the participants agreed, 19.9% disagreed, and 30% were undecided. However, only 20.6% of the total sample recalled the name of a document and only 4.1% of the respondents were able to list a correct or somewhat correct human rights declaration (UN human rights convention or UN human rights charter). The others gave names of incorrect documents, like the Charter of the UN (6.1%), UN documents (without any specification, 3.1%), the Geneva Convention (2.6%), the Basic Constitutional Law of the Federal Republic of Germany (3.5%), or The Bible/The Ten Commandments (1.3%).

Knowledge About Human Rights

Participants were asked (2002 study) to name all human rights they could recall spontaneously. On average, 3.03 single human rights were stated. On the level of single human rights, civil rights were listed much more often than economic rights ($M_{CR} = 2.22$; $M_{ER} = 0.81$; $p < .001$). The results were nearly the same when we analyzed the answers on the level of UDHR human rights articles. On average, participants listed fewer than 3 articles ($M = 2.78$). Again, articles dealing with civil rights were listed more often than articles dealing with economic rights ($M_{CR} = 2.05$; $M_{ER} = 0.73$; $p < .001$). The spontaneous listing of human rights revealed that only one single human right was known by more than one-third of the participants. This was the right to freedom of opinion and expression (Article 19 of the UDHR). Four additional human rights were named by approximately one-quarter of the participants. These were the right to life, human dignity, the right to freedom of religion, and the right to work. To put it differently, the spontaneous listing of human rights revealed a large lack of human rights education. Not one single human right was known by at least 50% of the sample. Furthermore, a distinct division between civil and economic rights was found. When human rights were recalled, they were mostly civil human rights.

However, the method of recalling a complex topic spontaneously might be too difficult for the participants. A person may have some knowledge about an issue like human rights but he or she may have difficulty recalling this by heart. Therefore, in the 2003 study we used the identification of rights as an additional method to assess knowledge about human rights. The results revealed that all civil human rights presented were identified by at least 50% of all participants as being *rather* or *certainly* a human right. The results regarding economic human rights were very different. Only two of the economic human rights presented were identified as human rights by at least 50% of the participants (right to free education in elementary schools; right to food, clothing, housing, and medical care). Four other economic rights were judged to be not a human right by the majority of the participants. Thus, the division between civil and economic rights can also be found using the identification method. Civil rights are identified as human rights with greater certainty than economic rights ($M_{CR} = 4.20$; $M_{ER} = 3.03$; $p < .001$). Moreover, when we analyzed the percentage of participants who rated a right as being *certainly* a human right, only six rights were identified correctly by more than 50% of the participants. These were, in descending order, the right to life and liberty (78.7%), the right to equality before the law (71.3%), protection against torture or cruel treatment (70.2%), protection against discrimination (69.3%), the right to freedom of opinion and expression (69.1%), and the right to freedom of religion (68.0%, see Table 1). These results also indicate major deficits in human rights education.

Importance of Human Rights

The realization of human rights for every human being worldwide was considered to be very important by the great majority (75.8%) of the participants (also, 18.6% rated *rather important* and only 1.3% *rather* or *very unimportant; M = 4.68; SD =* 0.65). Similar results had been found in the 2002 study, where we distinguished between the importance of specific rights (see Table 2). The majority of the participants rated most of the rights as being *very important*. Only three civil rights and four economic rights were rated as being *very important* by less than 50%. These were the right to freedom of religion, the right to seek asylum, the right to freedom of assembly, the right to participate in cultural life, the right to form trade unions, the right to limitation of working hours, and the right to protection against unemployment. The means for civil and economic rights show that economic rights are rated as slightly less important than civil rights ($M_{CR} = 4.41$; $M_{ER} = 4.32$; $p < .001$).

Commitment to Human Rights

In 2002, we assessed the expressed willingness to plead for human rights. Although a high percentage of the participants indicated a willingness to donate money to a hu-

TABLE 1
Identification of Rights as Human Rights in Descending Order of Means

Rights	Percentage Saying That According to the International Declarations of Human Rights, This Right is:					Means	SD
	Certainly Not a Human Right	Rather Not a Human Right	Don't Know	Rather a Human Right	Certainly a Human Right		
Civil human rights							
Right to life and liberty	2.3	2.1	2.8	13.8	78.7	4.65	0.67
Right to equality before the law	3.3	3.6	4.5	16.9	71.3	4.50	0.83
Right to freedom of opinion	3.6	5.4	3.1	18.7	69.1	4.45	0.98
Protection against discrimination	4.1	4.1	4.4	17.6	69.3	4.44	1.03
Right to freedom of religion	3.7	5.2	4.1	18.3	68.0	4.43	1.04
Protection against torture and cruel treatment	6.6	6.0	3.7	13.3	70.2	4.35	1.04
Right to seek asylum from persecution	5.0	8.3	9.9	27.7	48.5	4.07	1.17
Right to freedom of assembly	9.0	12.3	10.7	25.2	42.4	3.80	1.34
Protection against arbitrary interference with his privacy	11.3	14.0	9.1	23.2	42.1	3.71	1.42
Equal rights of men and women during marriage and its dissolution	15.2	13.5	10.1	19.0	41.9	3.59	1.51

Economic human rights						3.03	1.12
Right to food, clothing, housing and medical care	10.5	12.3	7.0	21.4	48.3	3.85	1.41
Right to free elementary education	18.9	16.1	8.6	19.0	37.1	3.40	1.56
Right to participate in cultural life	19.4	19.3	10.7	20.7	29.4	3.22	1.52
Right to social security	24.3	19.5	7.5	18.4	29.9	3.10	1.60
Right to equal payment for equal work	29.3	19.3	5.9	16.1	29.3	2.97	1.64
Right to form trade unions	26.4	20.8	14.5	18.3	19.6	2.84	1.49
Right to limitation of working hours and holidays with pay	37.3	21.7	8.0	16.3	16.1	2.52	1.52
Protection against unemployment	41.4	23.3	6.9	13.0	14.9	2.36	1.49
Distracting rights							
Right to peace	10.8	10.7	6.6	16.2	55.3	3.95	1.42
Right to abortion	36.9	23.7	13.0	13.3	12.5	2.41	1.42

Note. Rating scale: 1 (*certainly not a human right*) to 5 (*certainly a human right*).

TABLE 2
Importance of the Realization of Rights

Rights	Percentage Saying That the Realization of this Right is:					Means	SD
	Very Unimportant	Rather Unimportant	Neither Nor	Rather Important	Very Important		
Civil human rights							
Right to life and liberty	0.3	0.5	3.9	17.1	74.0	4.41	0.50
Right to equality before the law	0.2	0.9	4.8	17.3	72.7	4.71	0.59
						4.69	0.62
Right of freedom of opinion	0.3	0.5	4.7	19.8	70.5	4.67	0.62
Protection against discrimination	0.6	1.8	10.3	31.2	51.6	4.38	0.80
Right to freedom of religion	2.4	7.8	19.9	36.1	29.3	3.86	1.02
Protection against torture and cruel treatment	0.3	1.1	5.4	17.9	71.0	4.65	0.67
Right to seek asylum from persecution	1.8	3.9	20.4	30.6	39.1	4.06	0.97
Right to freedom of assembly	0.8	3.8	17.1	34.5	39.2	4.12	0.90
Protection against arbitrary interference with his privacy	0.3	0.9	7.4	21.9	65.0	4.57	0.70
Equal rights of men and women during marriage and its dissolution	0.4	1.2	9.3	26.2	58.7	4.48	0.75

	1	2	3	4	5	M	SD
Economic human rights						4.32	0.55
Right to food, clothing, housing and medical care	0.4	1.2	7.4	29.8	57.0	4.48	0.73
Right to free elementary education	0.4	1.8	7.1	22.9	63.7	4.54	0.74
Right to participate in cultural life	1.8	5.3	23.3	36.6	28.6	3.89	0.96
Right to social security	0.2	0.8	6.1	23.4	65.4	4.60	0.66
Right to equal payment for equal work	0.5	1.6	6.4	23.4	63.8	4.55	0.74
Right to form trade unions	1.8	6.5	21.6	34.3	31.3	3.91	1.00
Right to limitation of working hours and holidays with pay	0.9	2.6	13.5	34.5	44.1	4.24	0.86
Protection against unemployment	0.7	2.3	11.5	32.7	48.1	4.31	0.83
Distracting rights							
Right to peace	0.2	0.8	4.9	16.6	73.3	4.69	0.62
Right to intact environment	0.3	0.9	9.7	33.8	50.5	4.40	0.74
Right to denial military service	2.8	6.3	23.6	31.3	31.6	3.86	1.04
Right to abortion	3.1	5.9	25.3	33.7	27.4	3.80	1.03

Note. Rating scale: 1 (*very unimportant*) to 5 (*very important*).

man rights organization (49.2%) or to get actively involved in a human rights organization (44.7%), only a minority of these persons indicated they were *very willing* to do so (6% to spend money and 5.8% to get involved). We compared this expressed willingness with the actual behavior in the last 5 years, as declared by the participants in the 2003 study. According to the declared behavior, the sample was quite active: 24.5% *often* or *sometimes* supported human rights by signing petitions, 24.0% by donating money to a human rights organization, and 6.0% to having *often* (1.4%) or *sometimes* (4.6%) protested against human rights violations by taking part in a demonstration or picketing. Moreover, 4.3% indicated they had been actively involved in a human rights organization in the past 5 years. This comes close to, but is somewhat less than, the 5.8% who had indicated in the 2002 study that they were *very willing* to get actively involved in a human rights organization.

But what does it mean in more detail, if a person indicates his or her active involvement in a human rights organization? Of those persons who stated that they were involved in a human rights organization, 70.6% declared that they *often* or *sometimes* supported human rights in the last 5 years by taking part in a demonstration or picketing, signing a petition, or donating money to a human rights organization. Taking a closer look at those activities, we calculated that 32.6% of those persons who indicated their involvement in a human rights organization have actually protested against human rights violations by participating in a demonstration or picketing. That means that somewhat more than 1% of all participants have been actively involved in a human rights organization in the past 5 years and have *often* or *sometimes* protested publicly against human rights violations. It can be assumed that this 1% represents the core of those persons who are very committed to human rights protection. There might be another group of persons who are actively involved in a human rights organization but never participate in demonstrations or picketing. There also seems to be a relevant percentage of the population, which might be encouraged by specific campaigns, to donate money or to sign a petition.

EAST–WEST DIFFERENCES

East-West differences were calculated without using the weights, because the weights can not be applied to subgroups of the data set.

Differences in Knowledge About Human Rights and Human Rights Declarations

No East–West differences could be found regarding knowledge about human rights declarations. But there were differences concerning knowledge about specific human rights. West Germans were able to list more single civil rights and more articles dealing with civil rights than East Germans (Rights: M_{WG} = 2.40; M_{EG} = 2.04; $p < .001$; $\eta^2_{(rights)}$ = 0.010; Articles: M_{WG} = 2.23; M_{EG} = 1.86; $p < .001$; $\eta^2_{(articles)}$ = 0.013). However, East Germans were able to list more single economic rights and more articles dealing with economic rights than West Germans (Rights: M_{EG} = 1.09; M_{WG} = 0.55; $p < .001$; η^2 = 0.060; Articles: M_{EG} = 0.97; M_{WG} = 0.50; $p < .001$; η^2 = 0.058). The effect sizes show that the East–West differences regarding the spontaneous recall of economic rights were much greater than those concerning the recall of civil rights.

Similar results were obtained with the identification method. Although there were no East–West differences in the ability to identify civil rights (M_{EG} = 4.22; M_{WG} = 4.18; $p > .10$), East Germans identified economic rights more often as human rights than did West Germans (M_{EG} = 3.29; M_{WG} = 2.96; $p < .001$; η^2 = 0.013). The greatest East–West differences concerned the right to work, the right to education, the right to social security, and the right to peace. Table 3 lists all rights which showed East–West differences with an effect size of at least η^2 = .10, either for the spontaneous listing or the identification of human rights.

Differences in the Importance of Human Rights

When asked to rate the importance of human rights in general (2003 study), West Germans revealed only slightly higher ratings than East Germans (M_{WG} = 4.71; M_{EG} = 4.63; $p < .05$, η^2 = .003). A closer look at the two generations of human rights in the 2002 study shows that West Germans considered civil rights somewhat more important than did East Germans (M_{WG} = 4.43; M_{EG} = 4.34; $p < .001$; η^2 = .007). Economic rights, however, were considered more important by East Germans (M_{EG} = 4.40; M_{WG} = 4.29; $p < .001$; η^2 = .011). In a more detailed analysis, we investigated differences for specific rights (see Table 4 for all differences with an effect-size of $\eta^2 > .01$). The results reveal that West Germans evaluated two civil human rights as more important than East Germans: the right to freedom of religion and the right to asylum from persecution. However, East Germans considered four economic human rights as more relevant: the right to protection from unemployment; the right to equal payment for equal work; the right to food, clothing, housing and medical care; and the right to social security. They also rated one civil right (equality before the law) and one distractor item (right to peace, which is discussed as a human right of the third generation) as more important than did West Germans.

Differences in the Commitment to Human Rights

West Germans expressed greater willingness to donate money to a human rights organization (M_{WG} = 2.50; M_{EG} = 2.04; $p < .001$; η^2 = .065) and to get involved in a human rights organization (M_{WG} = 2.37; M_{EG} = 2.16; $p < .001$; η^2 = .013). However, in the subsequent study of 2003, we found no East–West differences concerning the active support of human rights in the past 5 years. The following section an-

TABLE 3
East-West Differences Regarding the Knowledge About Human Rights

		Means		
		East	*West*	η^2
Civil human rights				
Right to freedom of	Spontaneous listing	.22	.31	.011
religion	Identification	4.43	4.43	.000
Economic human rights				
Right to protection fro	Spontaneous listing	.37	.16	.057
unemployment	Identification	2.52	2.31	.003
Right to limitation of	Spontaneous listing	.02	.01	.001
working hours and	Identification	2.89	2.42	.014
holidays with pay				
Right to education	Spontaneous listing	.24	.11	.026
	Identification	3.66	3.02	.006
Right to participate in	Spontaneous listing	—	—	—
cultural life	Identification	3.56	3.13	.012
Distracting rights				
Right to peace	Spontaneous listing	.22	.22	.022
	Identification	4.23	3.89	.009
Right to abortion	Spontaneous listing	—	—	—
	Identification	2.78	2.37	.022

Note. Only those rights are listed, where an East-West difference in either the spontaneous listing or the identification of human rights with an effect-size of $\eta^2 \geq .01$ can be reported.

TABLE 4
East-West Differences Concerning the Importance of Specific Rights

	Means		
	East	*West*	η^2
Civil human rights			
Right to freedom of religion	3.57	3.95	.030
Right to asylum from persecution	3.91	4.11	.011
Right to equality before the law	4.78	4.66	.010
Economic human rights			
Right to protection from unemployment	4.53	4.26	.028
Right to equal payment for equal work	4.72	4.49	.027
Right to food, clothing, housing and medical care	4.62	4.44	.016
Right to social security	4.71	4.57	.012
Distracting rights			
Right to peace	4.82	4.66	.018

Note. All differences with an effect-size $\eta^2 \geq .01$ are listed.

alyzes whether the East–West difference regarding the willingness to actively work for human rights persists when other demographic and psychological variables are considered as well.

Factors Influencing the Commitment to Human Rights

To promote human rights education, it is relevant to know the variables that may influence the expressed willingness to support human rights, as well as actual supportive behavior. To analyze this topic, we conducted different stepwise regression analyses with each data set from the two representative studies. In the first step, several demographic variables (age, gender, income in household, and East–West) were entered into the regression analyses as predictors. In the second step, several potentially relevant psychological variables (knowledge about human rights, importance of human rights, authoritarianism, and SDO) were considered. In the 2002 study, the sum score of the two items dealing with the willingness to plead for human rights was used as the criterion. In the 2003 study, it was not adequate to build a scale consisting of all items pertaining to the active support of human rights. Thus, four separate regression analyses were calculated with each of the behaviors as the dependant variable.

Psychological factors played a significant role in explaining the variances regarding the support of human rights (see Table 5). Both knowledge about human rights and the importance of human rights showed a positive covariance with expressed willingness to support human rights and the self-indicated actual behavior. The beta weights were quite small. Another way of analyzing the data, however, showed the relevance of even these seemingly small effects. We formed three groups of nearly equal size according to the rated importance of the realization of human rights worldwide. With this procedure, the upper third showed relevant differences in their active behavior compared to the lower third, namely, 26.2% donated money (vs. 14.8% of the lower third), 27.4% (vs. 14.1%) signed petitions, and 6.9% (vs. 2.4%) took part in demonstrations or picketing.

Authoritarianism showed significant negative effects on active behaviors (donating money, signing petitions, and taking part in demonstrations or picketing) but no significant effect on the expressed willingness to plead for human rights. SDOs, however, showed only a significant effect on the expressed willingness. The higher the SDO, the lower is the expressed willingness to plead for human rights.

Concerning demographic variables, the results were mixed. Older people donated more money than younger people. Females signed more petitions than males. And finally, persons with higher formal education expressed greater willingness and declared more active behavior (signing petitions as well as taking part in demonstrations or picketing) than persons with lower formal education. The previously mentioned East–West difference regarding the willingness to plead for human rights remained stable in the regression analysis.

TABLE 5
Results of the Regression Analyses

	2002 Study		2003 Study		
	Willingness	Spend Money	Sign Petition	Demonstrate	Organization
First block					
Age	−.09**	.28**	−.01	−.10**	.03
Gender (1:men; 2:women)	.01	.06*	.10**	.03	−.02
Income of household	.06**	.06*	.07**	−.01	.04
Education	.12**	.03	.09**	.10**	−.04
West-east	−.21**	−.03	.02	.05*	.04
Second block					
RWA	−.03	−.06*	−.08**	−.16**	.09**
SDO	−.12**	.04	.01	.05	.00
Knowledge about HR	.20**	.09**	.07**	.09**	−.07**
Explanation of variance					
R^2 of first block	.11**	.09**	.03**	.03**	.01**
R^2 of second block	.07**	.01**	.02**	.02**	.01**
R^2-sum	.18**	.10**	.05**	.07**	.02**

Note. RWA = Right-wing authoritarianism; SDO = Social dominance orientations; HR = Human Rights.

DISCUSSION

Human rights are important topics in international politics. Because of the relevance of human rights, these studies examined what the general German population knows and thinks about human rights, and what people actually do to promote them.

Knowledge and Importance of Human Rights

These studies are the first ones in Germany, and probably worldwide, to examine the knowledge and the perceived importance of human rights using representative samples. A major result of these studies is that knowledge about human rights and about human rights declarations is quite poor. The name of the most relevant document—the Universal Declaration of Human Rights—is hardly known at all. Similar results have been found in the United States with a nonrepresentative sample (Hart Research Associates, 1997). In our studies, participants were also found to be able to name only very few specific human rights by heart. Not a single human right was named by more than half of the population. Only the right to freedom of opinion and expression (Article 19 of the UDHR) was spontaneously recalled by more than one third of the participants. Both of these results reveal great deficits in human rights education.

The knowledge about human rights appeared to be somewhat better when participants were asked to identify existing human rights from a list of different rights, indicating their degree of confidence whether an item was or was not a human right. If the vague answer "it probably is a human right" was counted as knowledge, the majority of the presented rights was identified by the majority of the participants. Analyzing the data this way, however, might include a lot of guesses in the category of "knowledge." If, however, only the more precise answer that a given right is "certainly a human right" was considered "knowledge," only one third of the human rights (6 out of 18) were identified correctly. This result might have been even less favorable if more human rights and more appropriate distracter items had been presented. The inclusion of the "right to peace" as a distracter item, for example, is debatable. The right to peace is not included in the actual Bill of Human Rights but it is part of the third generation and is a precondition for the realization of many human rights. Thus, we recommend that in further research, the right to peace and other rights of the third generation should not be used as distracter items.

Altogether, knowledge about human rights is inadequate. This result is relevant, especially if one takes into account the many attempts by UNESCO, as well as by the UN General Assembly, to proclaim human rights education as a very relevant topic to support democracy and peace.

A positive result of the representative studies is that the concept of worldwide realization of human rights, as well as the realization of many specific human rights, was evaluated as *very important* by the great majority of participants. This was true for civil rights as well as for economic rights, which is an important precondition for further human rights education.

However, in our study, some specific human rights (e.g., to seek asylum from persecution or to form trade unions) were not rated as being very important by the majority of participants. Furthermore, recent experimental studies show that there is an inconsistency between the support for general principles of human rights and the concomitant acceptance of violations of specific human rights (Staerklé & Clémence, 2004). It appears, therefore, that human rights education has to be more specific and to include more than the mere education of the knowledge of human rights.

Division Between Civil and Economic Rights and East–West Differences

Both the method of free recall and the identification of human rights point to another important aspect that we call the "division into half" between civil and economic rights. Civil and political rights are much better known than economic, social, and cultural rights. Similar results have been found in the U.S. sample (Hart Research Associates, 1997) and in a cross-national study of psychology students in Finland, Germany, Netherlands, Norway, and the former Yugoslavia (Sommer et al., 2004). All of these results contradict the demand made by the International Bill of Human Rights and by many conferences (e.g., Vienna World Conference on

Human Rights in 1993; cf. UN, 1995) that the different human rights are indivisible and interdependent.

This division between civil and economic rights might be understood as an aftereffect of the East–West confrontation, which dominated international politics for decades after the Second World War. One of the major ideological issues discussed in the West was that "the East violates human rights," especially civil and political rights. Economic, social, and cultural human rights were hardly discussed in this context. Thus, the social representation of human rights was generally restricted to political and civil human rights. The study by Sommer et al. (1992) has shown that the ideology of the division between civil and economic rights is promoted by German mass media. The analysis of human rights articles from all nationwide German newspapers (on the occasion of the 40th anniversary of the UDHR in 1988) showed that economic human rights were hardly mentioned. The human rights discussed were mainly civil and political rights. This is also reflected in politics. Up to this point, the United States has not ratified the International Covenant on Economic, Social and Cultural Rights of 1966. This is noteworthy, because the United States was very much involved in the development of the UDHR. , As early as 1941, during World War II, U.S. President Franklin D. Roosevelt stressed the importance of his four freedoms, including the freedom from want, which means economic security.

Therefore, the question arises what the psychological basis for the division in favor of civil rights might be. From a theoretical point of view, the division in favor of civil rights might be understood as the motivation to strive for a positive social identity. According to the social identity theory of Tajfel and Turner (1986), one way to obtain a positive social identity is to evaluate one's own group as superior to relevant other groups. Public opinion in Western countries emphasizes that democracies are more advanced in the realization of civil rights in comparison to China or Islamic states, for example. From this point of view, one can argue that Western countries stress civil and political rights because this is relevant for their identity.

The socialization and the identity enhancement interpretations are supported by the East–West differences. Our two representative studies have made it possible to compare East Germans and West Germans, who were separated by different ideologies for about 50 years. According to the knowledge about human rights, the greatest differences we found concerning economic human rights was that, compared to West Germans, East Germans could spontaneously recall and identify more economic rights. This could be interpreted as a socialization effect in different ideological systems. It is noteworthy that even though the knowledge about economic rights was greater in the East compared to the West, East Germans also differentiated between civil and economic rights. They recalled more civil human rights and identified them as human rights with more certainty than was true for economic human rights. The fact that 10 years after German unification, East Germans also differentiate civil and economic rights, might be the result of their motivation to strive for a positive social identity as "Germans."

Concerning the importance of human rights, the repeatedly found division between civil and economic rights in favor of civil rights was only found for the West German sample, which considered civil rights as more important than economic rights. However, East Germans rated economic human rights as more important than civil human rights. Although these differences are quite small, they also support the interpretation that ideological influences are still observable not only in the former socialist East Germany but also in the capitalist democratic West Germany. The strongest East–West differences concerning the importance of specific rights were found for the right to work (Article 23 of the UDHR). In socialist countries, the right to work has been emphasized as very important. The probable reason for this was the high unemployment rate in West Germany and other Western states. Because the East was criticized by the West for violating civil and political rights, the East could point to the violation of economic rights by the West. Another possible explanation for the East-West differences concerning Article 23 is the Protestant work ethic, which states that everyone gets what he or she deserves. The Protestant work ethic is much more common in the West than in the East. But there might be yet another reason for the observed differences concerning the importance of the right to work. Even more than 10 years after the unification of Germany, living conditions are quite different in East and West. The unemployment rate is much higher in East Germany, and wages are still lower. Therefore, these objective differences in daily life might contribute to the differences in knowledge about human rights and especially in the evaluation of economic human rights.

Human Rights Commitment

Concerning the commitment to human rights, nearly half of the population expressed their basic willingness to take part in actions. This percentage shrank heavily when the actual behavior shown in the past 5 years was considered. Nearly a quarter of the participants declared that they have signed human rights petitions *often* or *sometimes*, or have donated money to a human rights organization, and 6% indicated they *often* or *sometimes* protested against human rights violations by taking part in a demonstration or picketing. These might be correct numbers but they might also be an overestimation for methodological reasons. In the 2003 questionnaire, we asked for human rights commitment after we had presented a great number of possible human rights. For instance, a person might have protested against unemployment without being aware that the rights to work and protection against unemployment both are human rights. However, on the occasion of taking part in this study, he or she might have become aware that this behavior can be labeled as an effort to support human rights. Further studies should take into account this methodological problem.

Nevertheless, 1% of the population seemed to be the core of those persons who might be called activists in human rights protection. Although this number might look very small at first sight, translated into the German population it would correspond to about 650,000 people who are actively involved in favor of human rights. Furthermore, many more people are occasionally active. These people might be of special interest for further human rights education, because they represent a relevant potential for activities.

Criteria for Human Rights Education

A final aim of the two studies was to identify factors that influence the expressed willingness to support human rights and to promote human rights through actual behavior. Two factors have been identified as important variables: knowledge and the rated importance of human rights. The more people knew about human rights and the more they considered them as important, the more they expressed their willingness to get involved, and the more likely they were to take action. This means that, for human rights education, it is not only important to teach the contents of the Bill of Human Rights, especially the UDHR, but also to teach their general importance. Furthermore, it was assumed that RWA and SDO have a negative impact on human rights commitment. Against our hypotheses, RWA and especially SDO showed only weak and ambivalent effects. Thus, the results of a previous study (Stellmacher et al., 2003), where RWA and SDO had quite strong effects, can not be confirmed. This might be explained at least in part by the weak reliabilities of the utilized scales.

However, our representative studies were not designed to present and identify all factors that might be relevant for human rights education. Therefore, further research is needed to examine in more detail, and with specific subgroups, which psychological factors might improve human rights education and might lead to active behavior in support of human rights. Findings and theoretical background of research about political participation should be incorporated in such analyses. Research on social movements and politicized collective identity (e.g., Klandermans, 1997; Preiser, 2004; Simon, 2004; Simon & Klandermans, 2001) has identified a number of individual and social variables that help to understand the conditions under which people become politically engaged. Among these are adherence to values like human dignity or social justice, personal accountability, perceived probability of success, having a collective identity with shared grievances, as well as getting support by authorities or the general public. Moreover, the distinction of three kinds of motives that cause people to get involved in social movements could be helpful in explaining human rights commitment (see Klandermans, 1997, and for an overview, Simon, 2004, p. 161ff.): the collective incentive, which is derived from the value of the social movement's collective goals weighted by the perceived likelihood that these goals will be reached; the normative incentive, which is derived from the expected reactions of others weighted by the personal importance of these others' reactions to the potential participants; and the reward incentive, which concerns more personal and idiosyncratic gains or losses, such as losing money or time, making new friends, or risking the loss of one's friends.

PROSPECTS

The UDHR and subsequent documents define human rights as a guideline for political thinking and action and as a common standard of achievement for all peoples. However, human rights are still violated all over the world. There are not only human rights violations in countries like China, Indonesia, or Turkey, which are especially known for such violations from the Western perspective, but in Western countries as well. For instance, social and economic rights like protection against unemployment or equal pay for equal work are violated to a large extent. For example, four to eight million people (depending on the method of counting) are unemployed in Germany; and there is hunger, poverty, and homelessness in the United States (e.g., Brown & Allen, 1988). The economic approach of neo-liberalism ("globalization"), which is especially promoted by Western countries, often brings more instead of less poverty to developing countries (e.g., Stiglitz, 2002). The United States has played a direct or indirect role in human rights violations when they supported dictators in the Middle East and in Central and South America (e.g., Lykes & Liem, 1990). Even civil rights are in danger in Western countries. In Europe, for instance, the right to seek asylum from political persecution is severely restricted. Under the label of the "war against terrorism," many countries have already reduced or are presently reducing the individual freedoms for their own populations to a significant extent.

Furthermore, torture and other inhuman and degrading treatment of prisoners were applied by U.S. staff in the context of the wars in Afghanistan and Iraq. Moreover, in international affairs, the identification of, or the claim of, violations of human rights by one country have been used by other countries to justify political or economic sanctions. In recent years, even wars have been vindicated by claims of human rights violations, like the NATO war against the former Yugoslavia in 1999 (Sommer, 2001). This might be characterized as an abuse of human rights.

However, it is an aim of peace psychology to analyze national and international crises that have the potential to develop into violence, and to suggest possibilities for prevention or de-escalation of such conflicts (for recent overviews of peace psychology with major references to human rights, see Christie, Wagner, & Winter, 2001; Sommer & Fuchs, 2004). In this context, human rights are important as an ideal, which should be valid for all people in the world. Thus, human rights can be used as norms in evaluating societal and political conditions in different countries. One precondition for this is that everyone knows his or her rights. However, the two studies presented here show that there is a significant lack of human rights education in Germany. Other studies have shown that this holds true for other countries, too (see Hart Research Associates, 1997; Sommer et al., 2004). In accordance with the midterm evaluation of the UN decade for humans rights education, our results suggest that there is much to be done to achieve the central aims of human rights education, which are the promotion of knowledge about human rights, the detection of violations and abuse of human rights, the willingness to support human rights, and the empowerment to fight human rights violations.

ACKNOWLEDGMENTS

We thank Sarah Weiss for her assistance with the language and style of the text. We also thank three anonymous reviewers, as well as Klaus Boehnke and Richard Wagner, for their helpful comments.

BIOGRAPHICAL NOTES

Elmar Brähler, born 1946; diploma (MA-equivalent) in mathematics, 1970; Doctor of Human Biology, 1976, Professor since 1985; since 1994 Head of the Department of Medical Psychology and Medical Sociology at the University of Leipzig; Vice Dean of the Medical Faculty of the University of Leipzig since 2002. His research interests are health and social inequality (e.g., gender and migration), with a special focus on the subjective experience of health, health-care seeking behavior, family planning, reproductive health, and prenatal diagnostics; Member of the Reviewer's Board of the Deutsche Forschungsgemeinschaft.

Gert Sommer, born 1941, received his PhD in psychology from the University of Bonn, 1969; since 1977 Professor of Clinical and Community Psychology at the University of Marburg. His main research interests in the field of peace psychology are enemy images and human rights. For many years he has been president of the German Forum Friedenspsychologie (Peace Psychology) and member of the board of the journal Wissenschaft & Frieden (Science & Peace). In 2004, he received the Distinguished German Visionary Trophy by the Deutsche Gesellschaft für Verhaltenstherapie (German Society for Behavior Therapy).

Jost Stellmacher, born 1967, PhD in psychology at the University of Marburg in 2003. He is a scientific assistant in Professor Ulrich Wagner's social psychology workgroup at the University of Marburg. His main research fields are intergroup processes, ethnic prejudice, and human rights.

REFERENCES

Adorno, T. W., Frenkel-Brunswik, E., Levinson, D. J., & Sanford, R. N. (1950). *The authoritarian personality*. New York: Harper.

Altemeyer, B. (1996). *The authoritarian specter*. Cambridge, MA: Harvard University Press.

Annan, K. (2000). *Secretary-general says big gap exists between promises on human rights education and resources made available* (Press release SG/SM/7648/OBV/185). Retrieved June 10, 2003, from http://www.un.org/News/Preess/docs/2000/20001129.sgsm7648.doc.htm

Brown, J. L., & Allen, D. (1988). Hunger in America. *Annual Review of Public Health, 9*, 503–526.

Christie, D .J., Wagner, R. V., & Winter, D. D. (Eds.). (2001). *Peace, conflict, and violence: Peace psychology for the 21st century*. Upper Saddle River, NJ: Prentice Hall.

Doise, W., Spini, D., & Clémence, A. (1999). Human rights studied as social representations in a cross-national context. *European Journal of Social Psychology, 29*, 1–29.

Hart Research Associates. (1997). *Final adult survey data*. Retrieved August 19, 2003, from http://hrusa.org/hrmaterials/studies.shtm

Heitmeyer, W. (Ed.). (2002). *Deutsche Zustände (German conditions)*. Frankfurt a.M., Germany: Suhrkamp.

Klandermans, B. (1997). *The social psychology of protest*. Oxford, London: Blackwell.

Lykes, M. B., & Liem, R. (1990). Human rights and mental health in the United States: Lessons from Latin America. *Journal of Social Issues, 46, 151–165*.

Macek, P., Osecká, L., & Kostron, L. (1997). Social representations of human rights amongst Czech university students. *Journal of Community & Applied Social Psychology, 7*, 65–76.

Moghaddam, F. M., & Vuksanovic, V. (1990). Attitudes and behavior toward human rights across different contexts: The role of right-wing authoritarianism, political ideology, and religiosity. *International Journal of Psychology, 25*, 455–474.

Neumann, C., Evers, A., Sommer, G., & Stellmacher, J. (1999). Wissen und Einstellung bezüglich Menschenrechten im Verlauf eines Seminars [Human rights: Knowledge and attitudes in the process of a university course]. In G. Sommer, J. Stellmacher, & U. Wagner (Eds.), *Menschenrechte und Frieden. Aktuelle Beiträge und Debatten [Human rights and peace. Current contributions and controversies]* (pp. 356–363). Marburg, Germany: IAFA.

Ostermann, Ä., & Nicklas, H. (1979). Die halbierten Menschenrechte. Unterrichtsmaterialien zur Menschenrechtsdiskussion [The division in half of human rights. Educational materials for human rights discussion]. *Friedensanalysen, 9,* 115–159.

Petzel, T., Wagner, U., Nicolai, K., & van Dick, R. (1997). Ein kurzes Instrument zur Messung der Autorismusneigung [A short questionnaire to assess authoritarian disposition]. *Gruppendynamik, 28,* 251–258.

Preiser, S. (2004). Politisches Engagement für den Frieden [Political commitment to peace). In G. Sommer & A. Fuchs (Eds.), *Krieg und Frieden—Handbuch der Konflikt- und Friedenspsychologie [War and peace—Handbook of conflict and peace psychology]* (pp. 399–411). Weinheim: Beltz.

Sidanius, J., & Pratto, F. (1999). *Social dominance: An intergroup theory of social hierarchy and oppression*. New York: Cambridge University Press.

Simon, B. (2004). *Identity in modern society: A social psychological perspective*. Oxford, London: Blackwell.

Simon, B., & Klandermans, B. (2001). Politicized collective identity. *American Psychologist, 56,* 319–331.

Sommer, G. (1999). Die Menschenrechts-Charta der Vereinten Nationen—Kenntnisse, Einstellungen sowie Präsentationen in deutschen Printmedien [The human rights charter of the United Nations—Knowledge, attitudes and the presentation in German print media]. In G. Sommer, J. Stellmacher, & U. Wagner (Eds.), *Menschenrechte und Frieden. Aktuelle Beiträge und Debatten*

[*Human rights and peace. Current contributions and controversies*] (pp. 39–61). Marburg, Germany: IAFA.

Sommer, G. (2001). Menschenrechtsverletzungen als Legitimationsgrundlage des Jugoslawien-Kosovo-Krieges? [Human rights violations as a legitimization for the Yugoslavia-Kosovo war?] In J. M. Becker & G. Brücher (Eds.), *Der Jugoslawienkrieg—eine Zwischenbilanz [The war against Yugoslavia—interim result]* (pp. 81–92). Münster, Germany: LIT.

Sommer, G., Everschor, E., & Walden, K. (1992). Vierzigster Jahrestag der Allgemeinen Erklärung der Menschenrechte: Analyse deutscher Printmedien [The 40th anniversary of the Universal Declaration of Human Rights: An analysis of German print media] *Humboldt-Journal zur Friedensforschung, 8,* 19–28.

Sommer, G., & Fuchs, A. (Eds.). (2004). *Krieg und Frieden—Handbuch der Konflikt- und Friedenspsychologie* [War and peace—Handbook of conflict and peace psychology)]. Weinheim, Germany: Beltz.

Sommer, G., Stellmacher, J., & Brähler, E. (2003). Menschenrechte: Wissen, Wichtigkeit und Einsatzbereitschaft—Ergebnisse einer repräsentativen Befragung in Deutschland [Human rights: Knowledge, importance and commitment—Results of a representative study in Germany]. *Verhaltenstherapie & Psychosoziale Praxis, 35,* 361–382.

Sommer, G., Stellmacher, J. & Christ, O. (2004). *Cognitive representations of human rights in a cross national comparison.* Manuscript submitted for publication.

Sommer, G., & Zinn, J. (1996). Die gesellschaftliche Halbierung der Menschenrechte: Wissen, Einstellungen und Darstellungsmuster in deutschen Printmedien [The division in half of human rights: Knowledge, attitudes and presentation in German print media]. *Zeitschrift für Politische Psychologie, 4,* 193–205.

Staerklé, C., & Clémence, A. (2004). Why people are committed to human rights and still tolerate their violation: A contextual analysis of the principle-application gap. *Social Justice Research, 17,* 389–406.

Stellmacher, J., Sommer, G. & Imbeck, J. (2003). Psychologische Ansätze zu einer positiven Menschenrechtserziehung—Determinanten der Einsatzbereitschaft für die Einhaltung von Menschenrechten [Psychological Approaches to a positive human rights education—Determinants of the willingness to plead for human rights]. In E. H. Witte (Ed.), *Sozialpsychologie politischer Prozesse [Social psychology of political processes]* (pp. 143–166). Lengerich, Germany: Pabst.

Stellmacher, J., & Wagner, U. (1999). Entwicklung einer deutschsprachigen Skala zur sozialen Dominanzorientierung [Development of a German questionnaire for social dominance orientation]. Marburg, Germany, Unpublished report.

Stiglitz, J. (2002). *Globalization and its discontents.* New York: Norton & Co.

Tajfel, H., & Turner, J. C. (1986). The social identity theory of intergroup behaviour. In S. Worchel & W. G. Austin (Eds.), *Psychology of intergroup relations* (pp. 7–24). Chicago: Nelson.

United Nations. (1995). *The United Nations and human rights, 1945–1995.* New York: Author.

United Nations. (1999). *The right to human rights education.* New York: Author.

United Nations. (2002). *Human Rights—A compilation of international instruments.* New York: Author.

PEACE AND CONFLICT: JOURNAL OF PEACE PSYCHOLOGY, *11*(3), 293–312

Personal Values and Attitudes Toward War

J. Christopher Cohrs
Friedrich-Alexander University of Erlangen-Nuremberg, Germany

Barbara Moschner
Carl von Ossietzky University of Oldenburg, Germany

Jürgen Maes
University of the German Armed Forces, Munich

Sven Kielmann
University of Trier, Germany

Psychological determinants of generalized militaristic attitudes and attitudes toward specific wars were analyzed on the basis of 2 waves of a large German survey on attitudes after September 11, 2001 (Ns = 1,548 and 540). Personal values—as defined by the theory of basic human values by Schwartz (1992)—as well as ideological attitudes, threat of terrorism, and concern for human costs as mediators, were taken into account. Militaristic attitudes were consistently related to high priority of self-enhancement (power, achievement) and conservation (security, conformity) values and low priority of self-transcendence values (universalism, benevolence). Path analyses showed that the effects of conservation values were predominantly mediated by right-wing authoritarianism and threat of terrorism, and the effects of self-enhancement and self-transcendence values were predominantly mediated by social dominance orientation and (lack of) concern for human costs. These results suggest that there are 2 different psychological processes that lead to support for war.

In recent times, the world has witnessed several military interventions: the Kosovo War in Yugoslavia, the Afghanistan War against global terrorists and the Taliban regime, and the Iraq War against Saddam Hussein. What are the causes of such wars? Of course, a number of complexly interrelated factors are conducive to war,

---

Correspondence should be sent to Christopher Cohrs, Friedrich-Alexander University of Erlangen-Nuremberg, Social Psychology Section, Bismarckstr. 6, 91054 Erlangen, Germany. E-mail: crcohrs@phil.uni-erlangen.de

which are analyzed from different disciplinary perspectives, including history, political science, sociology, psychology, and biology. One of these factors is attitudes toward war in the public. Although public attitudes are influenced by policy makers and the media themselves, they can restrain foreign policy choices so that—at least in democracies—military intervention can only be carried out when there is support for or acceptance of war (e.g., Cunningham & Moore, 1997; Foyle, 2004; Sobel, 2001). Therefore, with attitudes being an important concept in psychology, one aim of peace psychology is to understand the psychological determinants of attitudes toward war. This article focuses on psychological determinants of war attitudes at different levels of specificity (cf. Cohrs & Moschner, 2002a). We take into account personal values at the most general level, ideological attitudes at an intermediate level, and war-specific feelings and beliefs at the most specific level. As dependent variables, we examine generalized militaristic attitudes as well as specific militaristic attitudes, that is, attitudes toward specific wars, namely, the Kosovo, Afghanistan, and Iraq Wars.

What did previous studies on psychological determinants of militaristic attitudes or attitudes toward war find? Concerning value determinants, most of the studies are based on the theory of basic human values by Schwartz (1992). This theory distinguishes ten motivational types of values that can be grouped into four broad categories of values, which contrast on two orthogonal dimensions: self-enhancement values (power, achievement) are opposite to self-transcendence values (universalism, benevolence), and conservation values (tradition, conformity, security) are opposite to openness-to-change values (hedonism, stimulation, self-direction). The 10 value types are arranged in a quasi-circumplex structure in such a way that adjacent values have similar motivational implications, whereas opposing values have contrasting motivational implications. It follows that associations between the 10 value types and external variables should decrease monotonically as one goes around the circular structure of values in both directions from the most strongly to the least strongly associated value type, so that a graphical representation of the correlations takes the form of a sinusoid curve. Attitudes toward war have been found to relate to self-enhancement and conservation values (e.g., Bègue & Apostolidis, 2000; Gordon, 1972; Johnson, Handler, & Criss, 1993; Mayton, Peters, & Owens, 1999). For example, in the study by Mayton et al. (1999), militaristic attitudes were correlated with high importance of power, achievement, hedonism, security, and conformity values. In the study by Bègue and Apostolidis (2000), positive attitudes toward the Kosovo War among French students related to high importance of conformity values and low importance of universalism values.

Concerning generalized ideological attitudes, early studies found militaristic attitudes to be embedded in an ideological syndrome that also includes nationalism, punitiveness, anti-communism, anti-internationalism, conservatism, authoritarianism, anti-democracy, ethnocentrism, and anti-Semitism (cf. Eckhardt, 1969, 1971, 1980). More recently, right-wing authoritarianism (RWA) and social domi-

nance orientation (SDO) have been identified as important determinants of attitudes toward war (e.g., Bartholomes et al., 1999; Cohrs & Moschner, 2002a,
2002b; Doty, Winter, Peterson, & Kemmelmeier, 1997; McFarland, 2005; Nelson
& Milburn, 1999; Pratto, Sidanius, Stallworth, & Malle, 1994; Stephan, Berger,
Schmidt, & Herrmann, 1995). These generalized attitudes are the two most powerful predictors of other political attitudes and generalized prejudice as well (e.g.,
Altemeyer, 1998; McFarland & Adelson, 1996; Van Hiel & Mervielde, 2002). Previous studies found that RWA relates to high priority of conservation (vs. openness-to-change) values and SDO relates to high priority of self-enhancement (vs.
self-transcendence) values (Altemeyer, 1998; Duriez & Van Hiel, 2002; Rohan &
Zanna, 1996), indicating that RWA and conservation versus openness-to-change
values, as well as SDO and self-enhancement versus self-transcendence values,
have similar motivational bases (see Duckitt, 2001).

At the level of war-specific determinants, a number of variables have been found
to influence militaristic attitudes. Cohrs and Moschner (2002b; see also Cohrs,
Maes, Moschner, & Kielmann, 2003) built on the theory of moral disengagement by
Bandura (1999). These and other authors (Grussendorf, McAlister, Sandström,
Udd, & Morrison, 2002; McAlister, 2001) argued that positive attitudes toward a
specific war are particularly likely when there is moral justification of the war (e.g.,
believing in worthy purposes such as humanitarian relief), denial or diffusion of responsibility for the war (e.g., seeing war as a last resort), blaming and dehumaniza-
tion of the enemy (e.g., portraying the enemy as dangerous, immoral, and guilty),
and negation or minimization of negative consequences of the war (e.g., ignoring human suffering). Other studies examined perceptions of threat from the enemy and
concern for human suffering (McFarland, 2005) as well as interests of the actor, relative power, perceptions of the enemy's motivations, and the enemy's culture
(Hermann, Tetlock, & Visser, 1999) as predictors of attitudes toward war.

Based on a comparable review of empirical results, Nelson and Milburn (1999)
concluded that militaristic attitudes are "nested within a value system and worldview
that gives high priority to the achievement and maintenance of power, authority, and
superiority for one's self and one's identity groups" (p. 161). In terms of the theory of
human values by Schwartz (1992), this conclusion basically refers to the dimension
of self-enhancement versus self-transcendence values. On the level of ideological
attitudes, SDO fits well into this pattern, and among war-specific determinants, lack
of concern for human suffering—as an expression of low universalism values—relates to this dimension. However, self-enhancement versus self-transcendence may
not be the only relevant dimension in war attitudes. Instead, determinants of militaristic attitudes such as conformity and security values, RWA, and feelings of
threat—as an expression of security values—also point to the significance of the
conservation versus openness-to-change dimension in Schwartz's (1992) theory.
Thus, predictors at all three levels of specificity support the notion that conservation
values are important as well.

Therefore, we hypothesize that both self-enhancement values and conservation values affect militaristic attitudes, and that these effects are mediated by different psychological processes. Specifically, self-enhancement values may operate through SDO and lack of concern for human suffering, whereas conservation values may act through RWA and feelings of threat from the enemy. This prediction will be tested with path analyses, thereby integrating determinants of militaristic attitudes on different levels of specificity. McFarland (2005) found support for parts of this prediction. He showed that, concerning prediction of attitudes toward the Iraq War, the effect of RWA, but not of SDO, was mediated by feelings of threat from Saddam Hussein, but the effect of SDO, but not of RWA, was mediated by lack of concern for human suffering.

METHOD

Overview

We analyze determinants of attitudes toward war on the basis of data from a study that we started shortly after the terrorist attacks on September 11, 2001. Most of the data was obtained via an Internet questionnaire; a minority of the participants filled out paper-and-pencil questionnaires. Because item and factor analyses yielded nearly identical results for the Internet and the paper-and-pencil samples, and both samples were similar in demographic characteristics (see Cohrs, Kielmann, Moschner, & Maes, 2002), the data were combined. Also, other studies found that data obtained through paper-and-pencil versus Internet questionnaires are generally comparable (cf. Gosling, Vazire, Srivastava, & John, 2004). We present cross-sectional results from the first (from October 2001 to January 2002) and the third (from September 2002 to March 2003) waves of data collection, in which personal values were assessed. For the analyses reported, we selected those variables that are particularly relevant for our research questions. For detailed information on the study, including the theoretical background of the measures, complete item wordings, and descriptive characteristics, see the technical reports (Cohrs et al., 2002; Cohrs, Kielmann, Maes & Moschner, 2003), which are available (in German) on the Internet (http://www.gerechtigkeitsforschung.de/berichte/).

Participants

We tried to obtain a demographically and attitudinally diverse sample by recruiting participants in various ways (e.g., via mailing lists, newsgroups, several societal organizations, Web sites, and the media; see the technical reports for more details). As incentives for participation, we offered feedback about the general results of the study and published a Web page with answers to frequently asked questions. At Time 3, we additionally offered a raffle of 5 × 50 Euros.

At Time 1, after deletion of double cases and cases with unusable or largely incomplete data, we obtained a sample of 1,597 cases. Participants were required to have answered at least 50% of the items of each construct used in the analyses. Remaining missing values were estimated by the expectation-maximization algorithm (see Schafer, 1997), separately for each of the constructs listed. This procedure resulted in a sample of 1,548 individuals, of whom 1,275 (82.4%) participated on the Internet and 273 (17.6%) filled out paper-and-pencil questionnaires. The percentage of men (53.2%, $n = 823$) was slightly higher than that of women (46.4%, $n = 718$; 7 participants did not reveal their gender). Age ranged from 14 to 75 years ($M = 30.53$, $SD = 10.70$). More than half of the participants were students (58.5%, $n = 905$). Overall, educational levels were high, as 918 participants (59.3%) had graduated from the German equivalent of high school (Abitur) and an additional 497 (32.1%) from university. The median time needed for filling out the Time 1 Internet questionnaire was 33 min.

At Time 3, the same procedure resulted in a sample of 540 cases, of which 273 cases (50.6%) were also in the Time 1 sample. The majority (97.4%, $n = 526$) participated over the Internet, 14 individuals (2.6%) filled out the paper-and-pencil questionnaire. Two hundred eighty-eight participants (53.3%) were men and 252 (46.7%) were women. Age ranged from 15 to 75 years ($M = 31.96$, $SD = 10.44$). About half of the participants were students (47.2%, $n = 255$). Concerning educational levels, 255 participants (47.2%) had graduated from the German equivalent of high school (Abitur) and an additional 228 (42.2%) from university. Ideologically, the sample was biased to the left. In the parliamentary elections in October 2002, 203 individuals (37.6%) reportedly voted for the Green Party, 103 (19.1%) for the Social Democrats, 50 (9.3%) for the Democratic Socialists, 41 (7.6%) for the Liberals, and 40 (7.4%) for the Christian Democrats; 86 participants (15.9%) did not provide an answer or said they did not vote.[1] The median time needed for filling out the Time 3 Internet questionnaire was 48 min.

INSTRUMENTS

Time 1 Measures

If not stated otherwise, for the following constructs items had 6-point response scales ranging from 0 (*full rejection*) to 5 (*full agreement*).

Personal values.   Values were assessed by the Portrait Values Questionnaire (PVQ; see Schwartz, 2005b; Schwartz, Melech, Lehmann, Burgess, Harris, & Owens, 2001), translated into German by the researchers, which is easier to administer over the Internet than the more commonly used Schwartz Value Survey (SVS;

---

[1]In the German political system, the Democratic Socialists, the Green Party, and the Social Democrats are typically considered left and the Liberals and Christian Democrats right.

Schwartz, 1992). Schwartz (2005b) as well as Bamberg, Herrmann, Kynast, and Schmidt (2003) presented evidence of reliability, relative stability, and construct and external validity of the PVQ, as well as convergent and discriminant validity of the PVQ and the SVS. Also, multidimensional analyses supported the quasi-circumplex structure postulated by the theory. The items consist of short descriptions of 40 persons. Participants had to rate how similar or dissimilar these persons are compared to themselves on 6-point scales ranging from 0 (*very dissimilar*) to 5 (*very similar*). All items of each type were averaged to scale values but one universalism item that implicitly refers to peace was discarded to avoid conceptual overlap with the dependent variables. Scale characteristics and exemplary items are presented in Table 1.

RWA.   We measured RWA by a 9-item scale developed by Petzel, Wagner, Nicolai, and van Dick (1997), which is a translation of items used by Altemeyer (1988). The scale has been validated in a number of studies (see Petzel et al., 1997). In our study, some items were replaced with the corresponding, clearer translations by Schneider (1997), and some items were modified linguistically. This slightly modified version had been validated in an earlier study by Cohrs and Moschner (2002a, 2002b). A sample item is: "To maintain law and order, tougher action should be taken against outsiders and troublemakers." Cronbach's $\alpha = .78$ ($M = 1.28$, $SD = 0.71$) in this sample.

SDO.   SDO was measured by a German translation of the 16-item scale by Pratto et al. (1994). Most items were taken from Six, Wolfradt, and Zick (2001) but some of their translations were adapted to make the items closer to the original meanings. An example item is: "It would be good if all groups were equal" (reverse-coded). In this sample, Cronbach's $\alpha = .89$ ($M = 1.67$, $SD = 0.72$).

Dependent variables.   All (translated) items used for operationalization of militaristic attitudes are presented in Appendix A. We assessed generalized militaristic attitudes with a modified 10-item scale that Cohrs (2000) assembled from various existing scales (e.g., Feser, 1972; Nelson & Milburn, 1999), Cronbach's $\alpha = .88$ ($M = 1.84$, $SD = 0.90$). Attitude toward the Kosovo War was measured by two items, Cronbach's $\alpha = .94$ ($M = 2.39$, $SD = 1.28$). Similarly, three items were used to measure attitude toward the Afghanistan War, Cronbach's $\alpha = .86$ ($M = 2.49$, $SD = 1.24$).

Time 3 Measures

If not stated otherwise, items measuring the following constructs had 6-point response scales ranging from 0 (*do not agree at all*) to 5 (*agree completely*).

Personal values.   Unlike at Time 1, we assessed personal values by a shortened version of the SVS to replicate Time 1 analyses with a more established value instrument. We used only the 45 items that had been identified as cross-culturally

TABLE 1
Values Scale Characteristics and Sample Items (Time 1)

Value Type	Sample Item	α	M	SD
Tradition	L thinks it's important not to ask for more than what you have. L believes that people should be satisfied with what they have.	.51	1.99	0.77
Conformity	It is important to J always to behave properly. J wants to avoid doing anything people would say is wrong.	.71	2.10	0.85
Security	It is very important to D that his or her country be safe. D thinks the state must be on the watch to threats from within and without.	.68	2.59	0.79
Power	B always wants to be the one who makes the decisions. B likes to be the leader.	.67	1.76	0.90
Achievement	Being very successful is important to W. W likes to impress other people.	.85	2.55	0.96
Hedonism	U really wants to enjoy life. Having a good time is very important to U.	.84	2.95	0.99
Stimulation	R likes surprises. It is important to R to have an exciting life.	.79	2.51	0.94
Self-direction	It is important to L to make his or her own decisions about what he or she does. L likes to be free to plan and to choose his pr her activities for himself or herself.	.60	3.82	0.64
Universalism	I wants everyone to be treated justly, even people he or she doesn't know. It is important to I to protect the weak in society.	.73	3.69	0.71
Benevolence	It is important to C to respond to the needs of others. C tries to support those he or she knows.	.63	3.45	0.65

valid by Schwartz (1992). Reliability and validity of this instrument has been widely documented, and multidimensional analyses supported the quasi-circumplex structure postulated by the theory (Schwartz, 1992, 2005a). Items were answered on 9-point scales, with categories labeled as −1 (*opposed to my values*), 0 (*not at all important*), and 7 (*of supreme importance*). All items of each type were averaged to scale values, with one universalism item ("A WORLD AT PEACE [free of war and conflict]") being discarded to avoid conceptual overlap with the dependent variables. Scale characteristics and exemplary items are presented in Table 2.

TABLE 2
Values Scale Characteristics and Sample Items (Time 3)

Value Type	Sample Item	α	M	SD
Tradition	HUMBLE (modest, self-effacing)	.53	2.34	1.33
Conformity	OBEDIENT (dutiful, meeting obligations)	.69	3.04	1.44
Security	NATIONAL SECURITY (protection of my nation from enemies)	.65	3.54	1.26
Power	AUTHORITY (the right to lead or command)	.66	1.79	1.38
Achievement	SUCCESSFUL (achieving goals)	.75	3.86	1.38
Hedonism	PLEASURE (gratification of desires)	.73	4.19	1.61
Stimulation	A VARIED LIFE (filled with challenge, novelty, and change)	.70	3.84	1.45
Self-direction	CHOOSING OWN GOALS (selecting own purposes)	.60	5.34	0.93
Universalism	SOCIAL JUSTICE (correcting injustice, care for the weak)	.71	5.04	1.02
Benevolence	HELPFUL (working for the welfare of others)	.69	5.23	0.96

Specific variables. To assess threat of terrorism, we used four items. An example is: "I don't feel that my everyday life is disturbed by terrorist attacks" (reverse-coded). In this sample Cronbach's $\alpha = .71$ ($M = 1.66, SD = 1.06$). To measure concern for human costs, we also used four items. A sample item follows: "Military action has led to tremendous suffering of innocent human beings." In this sample Cronbach's $\alpha = .80$ ($M = 2.64, SD = 1.13$).

Dependent variables. All (translated) items used for operationalization of militaristic attitudes are presented in Appendix B. We assessed generalized militaristic attitudes with 6 items from the scale used at Time 1. In this sample Cronbach's $\alpha = .87$ ($M = 2.03, SD = 1.06$). We assessed attitude toward the Afghanistan War by three items. In this sample Cronbach's $\alpha = .94$ ($M = 2.17, SD = 1.59$). Four items were used to measure attitude toward the Iraq War. In this sample Cronbach's $\alpha = .83$ ($M = 1.37, SD = 1.20$).

RESULTS

Time 1 Analyses

To examine the value correlates of militaristic attitudes, we computed partial correlations between the 10 value scales and the three kinds of militaristic attitudes, controlling for the average value rating as recommended by Schwartz (1992). This procedure is useful for methodological and theoretical reasons, as it controls for acquiescence and it is relative value priorities, rather than the absolute importance of values that is psychologically significant. The correlational pattern is presented in Figure 1. As predicted by the theory of basic human values, the curve has a perfect sinusoid shape, with the highest correlation with security and power values and the lowest correlation with universalism values. All three kinds of militaristic attitudes correlated significantly with high relative importance of security, power, conformity, and achievement values ($ps < .001$) and low relative importance of universalism and benevolence ($ps < .001$), as well as self-direction values (attitude toward Kosovo War: $p < .001$; generalized militaristic attitude and attitude toward Afghanistan War: $p < .01$). Further, attitudes toward the Afghanistan and Kosovo Wars correlated negatively with stimulation values ($p < .01$), and attitude toward the Afghanistan War correlated negatively with tradition values ($p < .01$). In sum, militaristic attitudes related to the self-enhancement versus self-transcendence dimension but also to the conservation values security and conformity.

Next, we analyzed in path analyses whether effects of values on militaristic attitudes are mediated by dual psychological processes. We hypothesized that self-enhancement versus self-transcendence values affect SDO, whereas conservation values influence RWA. Further, SDO and RWA should have an effect on militaristic attitudes. To obtain scores for conservation, self-enhancement, and self-transcendence value types, we averaged conformity and security values, power and achievement values, and universalism and benevolence values, respectively. The other values were not taken into account, as they did not relate substantially to militaristic attitudes. To evaluate model fit, we relied on two indexes: Root Mean Square Error of Approximation (RMSEA) and Standardized Root Mean Squared Residual (SRMR). According to Hu and Bentler (1999), RMSEA should be smaller than or close to .06 and SRMR should be smaller than or close to .08.

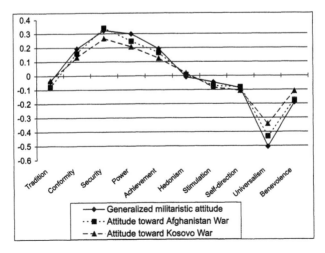

FIGURE 1   Partial correlations of values and militaristic attitudes at Time 1.

The hypothesized mediational model did not yield an acceptable fit to the data, $\chi^2(7) = 695.22, p < .001$, RMSEA = .25, SRMR = .16. Modification indices indicated that the residual variances of RWA and SDO were correlated, and that there were a number of unpredicted effects of values on RWA, SDO, and attitude toward the Afghanistan War. Freeing these paths resulted in the model presented in Figure 2. It fitted the data perfectly, $\chi^2(1) = 0.29, p = .59$, RMSEA = .00, SRMR = .00. All path coefficients were highly significant ($ps < .001$).

The predicted mediational processes were supported: The effect of conservation values on attitude toward the Afghanistan War was (partly) mediated by RWA, and the effects of self-enhancement and self-transcendence values were (partly) mediated by SDO. However, there were direct effects of all three value types on attitude toward the Afghanistan War, as well as effects of conservation values on SDO and effects of self-transcendence values on RWA. Thus, the two types of mediational processes were not clearly distinguishable. Nevertheless, RWA was affected more strongly by conservation than by self-transcendence values (CR [critical ratio] = 28.09, $p < .001$), and SDO was affected more strongly by self-transcendence than by conservation values (CR = 21.06, $p < .001$).

Equivalent path analyses were carried out for attitude toward the Kosovo War and generalized militaristic attitudes. Figure 3 shows the adjusted model for attitude toward the Kosovo War, $\chi^2(1) = 0.29, p = .59$, RMSEA = .00, SRMR = .00. Figure 4 shows the adjusted model for generalized militaristic attitudes, $\chi^2(2) = 5.90, p = .05$, RMSEA = .04, SRMR = .01. Here, conservation values had no direct effect on the dependent variable.

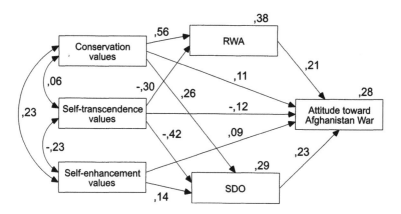

FIGURE 2   Path analysis to predict attitude toward the Afghanistan War at Time 1. Numbers are standardized path coefficients and explained variances. All coefficients are highly significant ($ps < .001$), except for the correlation between conservation and self-transcendence values ($p < .05$). Residual variances of right-wing authoritarianism (RWA) and social dominance orientation (SDO) correlate .42 (not shown).

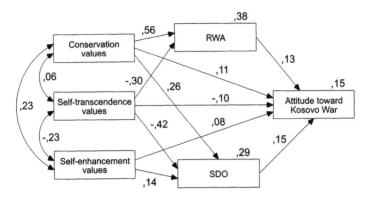

FIGURE 3   Path analysis to predict attitude toward the Kosovo War at Time 1. Numbers are standardized path coefficients and explained variances. All coefficients are highly significant (*ps* < .001), except for the correlation between conservation and self-transcendence values (*p* < .05). Residual variances of right-wing authoritarianism (RWA) and social dominance orientation (SDO) correlate .42 (not shown).

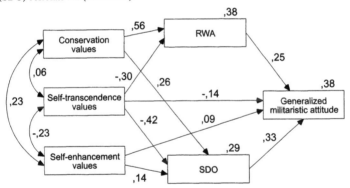

FIGURE 4   Path analysis to predict generalized militaristic attitude at Time 1. Numbers are standardized path coefficients and explained variances. All coefficients are highly significant (*ps* < .001), except for the correlation between conservation and self-transcendence values (*p* < .05). Residual variances of right-wing authoritarianism (RWA) and social dominance orientation (SDO) correlate .42 (not shown).

Time 3 Analyses

The correlational pattern of the personal values and the dependent variables is presented in Figure 5. Again, the average value rating was controlled for as recommended by Schwartz (1992). As at Time 1, the data formed a perfect sinusoid curve. Militaristic attitudes related to high priority of security and power values (*ps* < .001), as well as achievement values (generalized militaristic attitudes: *p* < .001; attitudes toward the Afghanistan and Iraq Wars: *ps* < .05) and conformity values (generalized attitude and attitude toward the Iraq War: *ps* < .01); and to low priority of universalism values (*ps* < .001), self-direction values (generalized attitude and

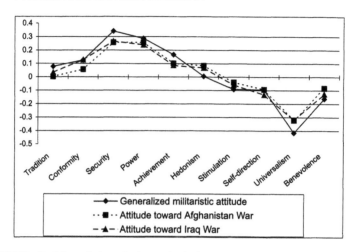

FIGURE 5   Partial correlations of values and attitude toward the Afghanistan War at Time 3.

attitude toward the Afghanistan War: $ps < .05$; attitude toward the Iraq War: $p <$ .01), and benevolence values (generalized attitude: $p < .001$; attitude toward the Afghanistan War: $p = .05$; attitude toward the Iraq War: $p < .01$). Thus, militaristic attitudes were predominantly related to the self-enhancement versus self-transcendence dimension but also to the conservation values security and conformity.

Next, we tested a path model in which values were used as distal determinants, threat of terrorism and concern for human costs as mediators, and attitude toward the Afghanistan War as the dependent variable. As threat of terrorism and concern for human costs were assessed specific to the Afghanistan situation, we did not carry out path analyses for generalized militaristic attitudes and attitude toward the Iraq War at Time 3. As at Time 1, we combined security and conformity values into a scale of conservation values, power and achievement values into a scale of self-enhancement values, and universalism and benevolence values into a scale of self-transcendence values.

In line with the assumed mediational processes, conservation values were specified to impact upon threat of terrorism, and self-enhancement and self-transcendence were specified to act upon concern for human costs. This model did not yield an acceptable fit to the data, $\chi(7) = 51.93, p < .001$, RMSEA $= .11$, SRMR $= .05$. Modification indices indicated that there were direct effects of conservation and self-transcendence values on the dependent variable. The resulting model fitted the data very well, $\chi^2(5) = 8.90, p = .11$, RMSEA $= .04$, SRMR $= .02$. It is presented in Figure 6.

Although conservation and self-transcendence values had direct effects on attitude toward the Afghanistan War, they had differential indirect effects. As expected, the indirect effect of conservation values was mediated by feelings of threat of terrorism, but not by concern for human costs, whereas the indirect effects of self-enhancement and self-transcendence values were mediated by concern for human costs but not by threat of terrorism.

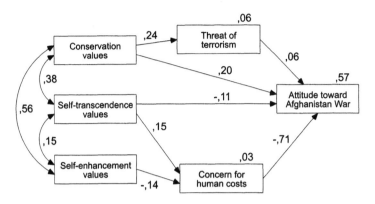

FIGURE 6   Path analysis to predict attitude toward the Afghanistan War at Time 3. Numbers are standardized path coefficients and explained variances. All coefficients are highly significant (*ps* < .001), except for the effect of threat of terrorism on attitude toward the Afghanistan War (*p* < .05).

DISCUSSION

This study investigated relationships between personal values and militaristic attitudes. The correlational results showed that militaristic attitudes relate consistently to low relative importance of self-transcendence values (universalism, benevolence) and to high relative importance of self-enhancement values (power, achievement) and conservation values (security, conformity). This pattern was independent of the instrument used to measure values, the PVQ or the SVS, and independent of the type of militaristic attitude used as a dependent variable—generalized attitude or attitude toward the Kosovo, the Afghanistan, or the Iraq War. Also consistently, universalism values were most strongly related to militaristic attitudes, followed by security values and power values. As a by-product, the theory of basic human values by Schwartz (1992) was supported by the sinusoid curves that represent the correlations. Because adjacent values have similar motivational implications, the magnitude of correlations decreases monotonically from the highest correlation into both directions around the circular value structure. In consequence, the conclusion by Nelson and Milburn (1999) that militaristic attitudes are linked to a personality system in which self-enhancement has high priority tells only part of the story and has to be refined. Concern for social conformity may be an additional, qualitatively different psychological source of militaristic attitudes.

The path-analytical results are somewhat less clear. Consistently and as predicted, the effects of conservation values on militaristic attitudes were partly mediated by RWA and threat of terrorism, and the effects of self-enhancement and self-transcendence values on militaristic attitudes were partly mediated by SDO and (lack of) concern for human costs. This suggests that the amplifying effects of self-enhancement (vs. self-transcendence) values and conservation values may result in part from different motivational processes. Militaristic attitudes may stem from a concern for power and superiority, which is reflected in SDO and a lack of concern for human suffering, and on the other hand, they may develop from a concern for security and social conformity, which is reflected in RWA and feelings of threat. This would be in line with the dual-process model of prejudice by Duckitt (2001; Duckitt, Wagner, du Plessis, & Birum, 2002). However, there were consistent direct effects of values on militaristic attitudes as well, over and above the effects of RWA and SDO or threat of terrorism and concern for human costs. Also, and more importantly, there were effects crossing the two different mediational processes: effects of conservation values on SDO, as well as effects of self-transcendence values on RWA. Nonetheless, these crossing effects were less strong than the effects within each mediational process. That is, conservation values act more strongly through RWA than through SDO and self-enhancement versus self-transcendence values operate more strongly through SDO than through RWA.

A clear demonstration of two distinct psychological processes that lead to militaristic attitudes is hampered by the fact that RWA and SDO were strongly related in our study. The correlation was .56, and other studies in European countries found correlations of similar magnitude (e.g., Aiello, Leone, & Chirumbolo, 2003; Van Hiel & Mervielde, 2002; Zick & Petzel, 1999). Thus, RWA may not be unambiguously related to the conservation (vs. openness-to-change) dimension, and SDO may not be unambiguously related to the self-enhancement versus self-transcendence direction (see Cohrs, Moschner, Maes, & Kielmann, in press). In consequence, it may be inadequate to use RWA and SDO as indicators of the assumed distinct motivational processes.

Another point related to the ideological attitudes RWA and SDO is that, although they have been found to be the two most important predictors of a range of political attitudes as well as explicit prejudice (Altemeyer, 1998; Duriez & Van Hiel, 2002; McFarland & Adelson, 1996), we found that values had additional effects over and above RWA and SDO, as well as threat of terrorism and concern for human costs, on militaristic attitudes. This is a clear demonstration that values are a most important concept in explaining political attitudes.

In our study, we took into account various types of militaristic attitudes at different levels of specificity and toward several specific wars. Further, we analyzed determinants of militaristic attitudes at different levels of specificity, thereby integrating different approaches to the explanation of attitudes toward war. However, the results presented in this article may not be cross-culturally valid but restricted to high-status, Western countries. This caveat is illustrated by a study by Levin, Henry, Pratto, and Sidanius (2003), in which aggressive attitudes toward an outgroup (the United States) increased with lower SDO scores in a Lebanese sample. Similarly, universalism values may not reduce militaristic attitudes in every culture. For example, valuing social justice, tolerance, and equality may be compatible with militaristic attitudes in cultures that feel oppressed and deprived of legitimate rights. Future cross-cultural studies should examine this idea. Generalization may also be limited due to the self-selection bias in terms of political ideology and educational level, which is typical for Internet studies. This bias can lead to restricted variance and, thus, lower correlations between values and attitudes. However, inflated correlations as a result of highly crystallized ideological attitudes and clearly structured attitude systems may also be expected (cf. Schoen, 2004).

What are the implications of our study? First, we showed—consistent with previous studies—that attitudes toward war are, in part, a function of generalized personality variables like values, RWA, and SDO. These variables are known to be quite stable over time (Altemeyer, 1998; Pratto et al., 1994; Schwartz, 2005b). Therefore, attempts of peace activism or peace education to reduce militaristic attitudes may be more successful when they are based on long-term considerations and deep-rooted personality variables are taken into account (cf. Nelson & Milburn, 1999). One method that may be useful in this regard is the value self-confrontation technique developed by Rokeach (1973), which tries to induce self-dissatisfaction by making people aware of inconsistencies in their system of values, attitudes, and behaviors (e.g., Grube, Mayton, & Ball-Rokeach, 1994). Second, educational attempts may be directed at two psychological themes. Because militaristic attitudes may stem from dual psychological sources—concern for power and superiority, as well as vulnerability to threat and concern for social conformity—it may be promising either to weaken needs for superiority and strengthen altruistic concerns, or to foster feelings of security and personal autonomy.

BIOGRAPHICAL NOTES

Christopher Cohrs, born 1974, studied psychology at the University of Bielefeld, where he also received his PhD. He works in the Social Psychology Section at the Friedrich-Alexander University of Erlangen-Nuremberg. His current research is on (a) ideology, threat, and prejudice, (b) patriotism and commitment against right-wing extremism, and (c) attitudes toward war.

Barbara Moschner, born 1961, studied psychology at the University of Trier, where she also received her doctoral degree. She works as a professor in the School of Education at Carl von Ossietzky University of Oldenburg. Her current research is on (a) epistemological beliefs; (b) self-concept, motivation, and learning strategies; and (c) educational reconstruction.

Jürgen Maes, born 1958, received his diploma in psychology and his doctoral degree from the University of Trier, where he worked in the Educational and Applied Psychology Section. He is now working as a professor in the Faculty of Education at the University of the German Armed Forces in Munich. His current research is on (a) the justice motive, (b) learning processes, and (c) social responsibility.

Sven Kielmann, born 1973, received his diploma in psychology from the University of Trier. His research interests lie in (a) social and applied psychology and (b) online research and its methodology.

REFERENCES

Aiello, A., Leone, L., & Chirumbolo, A. (2003, July). *Validation of the utility of social dominance orientation in Italy*. Paper presented at the 26th Annual Meeting of the International Society of Political Psychology, Boston, MA.

Altemeyer, B. (1988). *Enemies of freedom. Understanding right-wing authoritarianism*. San Francisco, CA: Jossey-Bass.

Altemeyer, B. (1998). The other "authoritarian personality". In M. P. Zanna (Ed.), *Advances in experimental social psychology* (Vol. 30, pp. 47–92). San Diego, CA: Academic Press.

Bamberg, S., Herrmann, J., Kynast, S., & Schmidt, P. (2003). *"Portraits Questionnaire"—Ein neues Instrument zur Messung von Schwartz "Theorie grundlegender menschlicher Werte"* [*"Portraits Questionnaire"—A new instrument to measure Schwartz' "theory of basic human values"*]. Unpublished manuscript, University of Gleben, Germany.

Bandura, A. (1999). Moral disengagement in the perpetration of inhumanities. *Personality and Social Psychology Bulletin, 3*, 193–209.

Bartholomes, S., Gericke, G., Hartenstein, S., Hübner, T., Joseph, A., Stössl, K., et al. (1999, July 27). *Autoritarismus und Kosovokonflikt—Eine Internetstudie* [Authoritarianism and Kosovo conflict—An Internet study]. Retrieved June 21, 2000, from http://www.uni-jena.de/~sff/research/kosovo_net_a3.pdf.

Bègue, L., & Apostolidis, T. (2000). The 1999 Balkan war: Changes in ratings of values and prowar attitudes among French students. *Psychological Reports, 86*, 1127–1133.

Cohrs, J. C., Kielmann, S., Maes, J., & Moschner, B. (2003). *Befragung zum 11. September und den Folgen: Bericht über die dritte Erhebungsphase* [Survey on September 11 and the consequences: Report on the third wave of data collection] (Reports from the working group "Verantwortung, Gerechtigkeit, Moral", No. 160). Trier, Germany: University of Trier, Faculty I—Psychology.

Cohrs, J. C., Kielmann, S., Moschner, B., & Maes, J. (2002). *Befragung zum 11. September 2001 und den Folgen: Grundideen, Operationalisierungen und deskriptive Ergebnisse der ersten Erhebungsphase* [Survey on September 11 and the consequences: Basic ideas, operationalizations, and descriptive results of the first wave of data collection] (Reports from the working group "Verantwortung, Gerechtigkeit, Moral", No. 148). Trier, Germany: University of Trier, Faculty I—Psychology.

Cohrs, J. C., Maes, J., Moschner, B., & Kielmann, S. O. (2003). Patterns of justification of the United States' "war against terrorism" in Afghanistan. *Psicología Política, 27*, 105–117.

Cohrs, J. C., & Moschner, B. (2002a). Antiwar knowledge and generalized political attitudes as determinants of attitude toward the Kosovo War. *Peace and Conflict: Journal of Peace Psychology, 8*, 141–157.

Cohrs, J. C., & Moschner, B. (2002b). Zur kognitiven Konstruktion von (Un-)Gerechtigkeit militärischer Gewalt: Die moralische Beurteilung des Kosovo-Kriegs [Cognitive construction of the (un-)justness of military force: The moral evaluation of the Kosovo War]. *Zeitschrift für Sozialpsychologie, 33*, 13–24.

Cohrs, J. C., Moschner, B., Maes, J., & Kielmann, S. (in press). The motivational bases of right-wing authoritarianism and social dominance orientation: Relations to values and attitudes in the aftermath of September 11, 2001. *Personality and Social Psychology Bulletin*.

Cunningham, J., & Moore, M. K. (1997). Elite and mass foreign policy opinions: Who is leading this parade? *Social Science Quarterly, 78,* 641–656.

Doty, R. M., Winter, D. G., Peterson, B. E., & Kemmelmeier, M. (1997). Authoritarianism and American students' attitudes about the Gulf War, 1990–1996. *Personality and Social Psychology Bulletin, 23,* 1133–1143.

Duckitt, J. (2001). A dual-process cognitive-motivational theory of ideology and prejudice. In M. P. Zanna (Ed.), *Advances in experimental social psychology* (Vol. 33, pp. 41–113). San Diego, CA: Academic Press.

Duckitt, J., Wagner, C., du Plessis, I., & Birum, I. (2002). The psychological bases of ideology and prejudice: Testing a dual process model. *Journal of Personality and Social Psychology, 83,* 75–93.

Duriez, B., & Van Hiel, A. (2002). The march of modern fascism: A comparison of social dominance orientation and authoritarianism. *Personality and Individual Differences, 32,* 1199–1213.

Eckhardt, W. (1969). The factor of militarism. *Journal of Peace Research, 6,* 123–132.

Eckhardt, W. (1971). Cross-cultural militarism: A test of Krieger's developmental model of military man. *Journal of Contemporary Revolutions, 3*(2), 113–139.

Eckhardt, W. (1980). The causes and correlates of Western militarism. In A. Eide & M. Thee (Eds.), *Problems of contemporary militarism* (pp. 323–355). New York: St. Martin.

Feser, H. (1972). *Erfassung von Militarismus-Pazifismus bei Jugendlichen* [Measurement of militarism-pacifism in adolescents]. Unpublished doctoral dissertation, University of Würzburg, Germany.

Foyle, D. C. (2004). Leading the public to war? The influence of American public opinion on the Bush administration's decision to go to war in Iraq. *International Journal of Public Opinion Research, 16,* 269–294.

Gordon, L. V. (1972). Value correlates of student attitudes on social issues: A multination study. *Journal of Applied Psychology, 56,* 305–311.

Gosling, S. D., Vazire, S., Srivastava, S., & John, O. P. (2004). Should we trust Web-based studies? A comparative analysis of six preconceptions about Internet questionnaires. *American Psychologist, 59,* 93–104.

Grube, J. W., Mayton, D. M., & Ball-Rokeach, S. J. (1994). Inducing change in values, attitudes, and behaviors: Belief system theory and the method of value self-confrontation. *Journal of Social Issues, 50*(4), 153–173.

Grussendorf, J., McAlister, A., Sandström, P., Udd, L., & Morrison, T. C. (2002). Resisting moral disengagement in support for war: Use of the "peace test" scale among student groups in 21 nations. *Peace and Conflict: Journal of Peace Psychology, 8,* 73–83.

Herrmann, R. K., Tetlock, P. E., & Visser, P. S. (1999). Mass public decisions to go to war: A cognitive-interactionist framework. *American Political Science Review, 93,* 553–573.

Hu, L., & Bentler, P. M. (1999). Cutoff criteria for fit indexes in covariance structure analysis: Conventional criteria versus new alternatives. *Structural Equation Modeling, 6,* 1–55.

Johnson, P. B., Handler, A., & Criss, J. E. (1993). Beliefs related to acceptance of war. In K. Larsen (Ed.), *Conflict and social psychology* (pp. 225–240). London: Sage.

Levin, S., Henry, P. J., Pratto, F., Sidanius, J. (2003). Social dominance and social identity in Lebanon: Implications for support of violence against the West. *Group Processes and Intergroup Relations, 6,* 353–368.

Mayton, D. M., Peters, D. J., & Owens, R. W. (1999). Values, militarism, and nonviolent predispositions. *Peace and Conflict: Journal of Peace Psychology, 5,* 69–77.

McAlister, A. L. (2001). Moral disengagement: Measurement and modification. *Journal of Peace Research, 38,* 87–99.

McFarland, S. G. (2005). On the eve of war: Authoritarianism, social dominance, and American students' attitudes toward attacking Iraq. *Personality and Social Psychology Bulletin, 31,* 360–367.

McFarland, S., & Adelson, S. (1996, June/July). *An omnibus study of personality and prejudice.* Paper presented at the Annual Scientific Meeting of the International Society of Political Psychology, Vancouver, Canada.

Nelson, L. L., & Milburn, T. W. (1999). Relationships between problem-solving competencies and militaristic attitudes: Implications for peace education. *Peace and Conflict: Journal of Peace Psychology, 5,* 149–168.

Petzel, T., Wagner, U., Nicolai, K., & van Dick, R. (1997). Ein kurzes Instrument zur Messung der Autoritarismus-Neigung [A short instrument to measure authoritarian tendency]. *Gruppendynamik, 28,* 251–258.

Pratto, F., Sidanius, J., Stallworth, L. M., & Malle, B. F. (1994). Social dominance orientation: A personality variable predicting social and political attitudes. *Journal of Personality and Social Psychology, 67,* 741–763.

Rohan, M. J., & Zanna, M. P. (1996). Value transmissions in families. In C. Seligman, J. M. Olson, & M. P. Zanna (Eds.), *The psychology of values* (pp. 253–276). Mahwah, NJ: Lawrence Erlbaum Associates, Inc.

Rokeach, M. (1973). *The nature of human values.* New York: Free Press.

Schafer, J. (1997). *Analysis of incomplete multivariate data.* London: Chapman & Hall.

Schneider, J. F. (1997). Erfahrungen mit deutschsprachigen Versionen der Right-Wing Authoritarianism Scale von Altemeyer [Experiences with German versions of the Right-Wing Authoritarianism Scale by Altemeyer]. *Gruppendynamik, 28,* 239–249.

Schoen, H. (2004). Online-Umfragen—Schnell, billig, aber auch Valide? Ein vergleich zweier Internetbefragungen mit persönlichen Interviews zur Bundestagswahl 2002 [Online surveys—Fast, cheap, but also valid? A comparison of two Internet surveys with personal interviews on the German federal election 2002]. *ZA-Information, 54,* 27–52.

Schwartz, S. H. (1992). Universals in the content and structure of values: Theoretical advances and empirical tests in 20 countries. In M. P. Zanna (Ed.), *Advances in experimental social psychology* (Vol. 25, pp. 1–65). San Diego, CA: Academic Press.

Schwartz, S. H. (2005a). Basic human values: Their content and structure across cultures. In A. Tamayo & J. B. Porto (Eds.), *Valores e compartamento nas organizacións* [Values and behaviors in organizations]. Petropolis, Brasilia: Vozes.

Schwartz, S. H. (2005-b). Robustness and fruitfulness of a theory of universals in individual human values. In A. Tamayo & J. B. Porto (Eds.), *Valores e compartamento nas organizacións* [Values and behaviors in organizations]. Petropolis, Brasilia: Vozes.

Schwartz, S. H., Melech, G., Lehmann, A., Burgess, S., Harris, M., & Owens, V. (2001). Extending the cross-cultural validity of the theory of basic human values with a different method of measurement. *Journal of Cross-Cultural Psychology, 32,* 519–542.

Six, B., Wolfradt, U., & Zick, A. (2001). Autoritarismus und Soziale Dominanzorientierung als generalisierte Einstellungen [Authoritarianism and social dominance orientation as generalized attitudes]. *Zeitschrift für Politische Psychologie, 9,* 23–40.

Sobel, R. (2001). *The impact of public opinion on U.S. foreign policy since Vietnam. Constraining the colossus.* New York: Oxford University Press.

Stephan, K., Berger, M., Schmidt, P., & Herrmann, A. (1995). Die Deutschen und der Golfkrieg [The Germans and the Gulf War]. In G. Lederer & P. Schmidt (Eds.), *Autoritarismus und Gesellschaft* [*Authoritarianism and society*] (pp. 250–286). Opladen, Germany: Leske + Budrich.

Van Hiel, A., & Mervielde, I. (2002). Explaining conservative beliefs and political preferences: A comparison of social dominance orientation and authoritarianism. *Journal of Applied Social Psychology, 32,* 965–976.

Zick, A., & Petzel, T. (1999). Authoritarianism, racism, and ideologies about acculturation. *Politics, Groups, and the Individual, 8,* 41–64.

APPENDIX A
Items on Militaristic Attitudes at Time 1

Item	M	SD	r_{iT}
Generalized Militaristic Attitude			
People can live without arms and war on this earth.[a]	1.85	1.44	.56
Our state should spend much less on armaments.[a]	1.80	1.39	.65
One should seriously consider to also use the military in domestic conflicts.	0.65	0.98	.42
War is an indispensable means to solve international conflicts.	1.17	1.16	.70
War is a crime against life and therefore morally reprehensible.[a]	1.28	1.22	.67
In some cases, war can be justified to maintain justice.	2.58	1.29	.69
Unfortunately, war is unavoidable due to human nature.	2.42	1.39	.55
War is never justified.[a]	2.01	1.45	.73
Threat of military force is often the best way to keep down aggressive states.	2.22	1.24	.61
Only the militarily strong can negotiate successfully in international conflicts.	2.43	1.25	.54
Attitude toward the Kosovo War			
I am of the opinion that by and large, NATO's military action in Kosovo in 1999 was justified.	2.34	1.30	.89
In my opinion it was wrong of NATO to intervene militarily in Kosovo in 1999.[a]	2.44	1.34	.89
Attitude toward the Afghanistan War			
Under no circumstances should there be military actions against the terrorists.[a]	2.77	1.39	.76
Action should be taken against the terrorist and their supporters through all available military means.	1.78	1.47	.73
There should be military actions against those immediately responsible.	2.94	1.37	.72

[a]Reverse-coded items; high values indicate militaristic responses.

Items on Militaristic Attitudes at Time 3

Item	M	SD	r_{iT}
Generalized Militaristic Attitude			
Our state should spend much less on armaments.[a]	1.72	1.41	.63
War is a crime against life and therefore morally reprehensible.[a]	1.28	1.24	.71
In some cases, war can be justified to maintain justice.	2.52	1.34	.70
War is never justified.[a]	2.01	1.51	.75
Threat of military force is often the best way to keep down aggressive states.	2.24	1.27	.67
Only the militarily strong can negotiate successfully in international conflicts.	2.42	1.37	.56
Attitude toward the Afghanistan War			
I firmly reject the military intervention in Afghanistan.[a]	2.34	1.69	.90
By and large, I consider the military action in Afghanistan justified.	2.15	1.67	.87
The military intervention in Afghanistan clearly went beyond a justifiable degree.[a]	2.02	1.71	.83
Attitude toward the Iraq War			
It would be justified to take military action against Iraq.	0.86	1.17	.76
Under no circumstances should the United States go to war against Iraq.[a]	1.07	1.48	.64
Iraq should be forced to accept UN weapons inspections—if necessary by military means.	2.14	1.68	.64
If necessary, Saddam Hussein should be brought down with military force.	1.42	1.52	.67

[a]Reverse-coded items; high values indicate militaristic responses.

PEACE AND CONFLICT: JOURNAL OF PEACE PSYCHOLOGY, *11*(3), 313–336

Social Identity in Times of International Conflict

Michaela Kolbe and Margarete Boos
University of Goettingen

Andrea Gurtner
Université de Neuchatel

Given the strained political situation in Iraq and general unrest in the world, in two studies we asked adolescents not directly involved in the Iraqi crisis about their identification with their particular nation, with Europeans, and as citizens of the world. We explored their fears and predicted changes in the face of a possible war in Iraq. Additionally, we asked the students about their political attitudes and related them to their reported changes and expectations and degrees of identification. Study 2 also investigated whether students from 3 different countries holding differing official opinions on the Iraqi crisis (Germany, Switzerland, Spain) differed in their national identification and in their attitudes, fears, and expectations.

Results show only moderate levels of student identification with their nations. The exception is Spain, in Study 2, where the Spanish students highly identify with being Spanish. The reported fears and changes in face of war are manifold and range from fears of insecurity and terrorist attacks, rising political and religious tension, to worries concerning rising petrol prices. Most of the students did not support a military intervention in Iraq. Differences between the students in the three countries and their relation to social identification are discussed.

THE IRAQI CRISIS AND INTERNATIONAL DEBATE OVER INTERVENTION

As 2002 drew to a close, the crisis in Iraq and the international debate regarding military intervention shaped everyday life and exacerbated the uncertainty of peace in the world. In November 2002, the United Nations passed a resolution to force Iraq to give up weapons of mass destruction, threatening serious consequences in the event

Correspondence should be sent to Michaela Kolbe, Department of Social Psychology and Communication Studies, Institute of Psychology, Gosslerstrasse 14, 37073 Goettingen, Germany. E-mail: mkolbe@uni_goettingen.de

of noncompliance. Four months later, no weapons of mass destruction had been found and the weapon inspections were declared unsuccessful in achieving the disarmament of Iraq. The outbreak of war seemed likely, with or without UN approval, spawning international opposition and warning against a military intervention (Ramsay, 2002). Some European states (e.g., France and Germany) expressed severe doubts about the wisdom of an armed intrusion into Iraq. There were massive demonstrations against the war in major cities all over the world, including cities in the two nations spearheading the intervention—Great Britain and the United States.

The aim of our two studies was not only to present fears that young people reported in the face of war in Iraq but also to illustrate how they experienced a situation of rising international tension, particularly with regard to their social identification and political attitudes. In the context of looming war, these studies examine social identity and collective self-esteem in adolescents who normally live in peaceful circumstances and now have to deal with the probability of war and its unpredictable impact on their lives. An additional element is the uncertainty about the use of nuclear weapons in the event of war, which could cause fear across the globe. Poilkolainen, Kanerva, and Lönnqvist (1998) confirmed that the threat of modern warfare can lead to fear even among young people who live far from the area of conflict.

THE SITUATION IN GERMANY

The sociopolitical situation in Germany before the outbreak of war in Iraq can be described as complex and problematic regarding this international crisis. Germans felt divided for or against a military intervention in Iraq—a severe dissension that played an essential role during the election campaign in autumn 2002. Despite this division, all Germans felt affronted by the criticism of their officially declared rejection of military intervention by the proponents of war, in particular Great Britain and the United States. Because of this widely reported political division, it can be assumed that Germans, especially younger Germans, felt insecure about their political affiliations and about the appropriateness of their general political attitudes (e.g., holding a pacifist attitude).

WHY ANALYZE IDENTITY, POLITICAL ATTITUDE, AND FEARS IN ADOLESCENTS?

Adolescence is regarded as a period of time when beliefs about the self are refined and a feeling of identity develops (Makros & McCabe, 2001; Marcia, 1980). The process of identity formation implicates an interplay between external and internal aspects (Makros & McCabe, 2001). Identity development occurs in a cultural context and has been seen as one of the main tasks of the passage into adulthood (Erikson, 1950, 1968). Schwartz and Montgomery (2002) discussed the complexity of the identity development process, which depends on specific identity components, as well as the context of this development. Next to personal identity, individuals also strive to achieve positive social identity derived from the social categories to which they perceive themselves belonging (Tajfel & Turner, 1986; Turner, 1985). Martinez and Dukes (1997) emphasize the importance of ethnic identity in adolescents for their well being (e.g., self-esteem and purpose in life). They found that an increase in ethnic identity results in an increase in psychological well being. In the given context of war and political tension, we regard identification with different political categories as especially crucial to development of social and national identity. Several studies have concentrated on adolescents who live with enduring war and political conflicts and their relation to psychological well being and self-esteem (e.g., Elbedour, 1998; Stringer, Cornish, & Denver, 2000). Elbedour (1998) found that violence, warlike conditions, and extreme social change influenced mental health adjustment of Gaza Palestinian, Israeli Bedouin Arab, and Israeli Jewish adolescents. In Northern Ireland, Stringer et al. (2000) found that attitudes, perceptions, and preferences for locations among Northern Ireland students differed in dependence on peace time versus periods of intergroup conflict. The purpose of our studies is to investigate young people who are not directly involved in the Iraqi crisis and its consequences. Do they nevertheless report threats and anxiety? Do they regard the Iraqi crisis as crucial for world peace? And, regarding feelings of belonging and social integration, with whom do they identify?

THE CRUCIAL ROLE OF IDENTIFICATION

The role of ingroup identification in social perception and behavior is processed by social identity theory (Tajfel & Turner, 1986) and self-categorization theory (Turner et al., 1987). The social identity perspective analyzes groups with regard to their members' sense of belonging and identification (Poole, Hollingshead, McGrath, Moreland, & Rohrbaugh, 2004). Social identity as a construct is based on group identification and influences the dynamics between groups. Identification can be considered a multidimensional concept (Jackson, 2002; Kashima, Kashima, & Hardie, 2000) which reflects one's general psychological affiliation with one's ingroup. The underlying dimensions are cognitive (e.g., perceived similarity between self and ingroup); and affective-evaluative—emotional reactions to one's group membership described through group identification (Kashima et al., 2000; Tropp & Wright, 1999). Tropp and Wright (2001) define ingroup identification as "the degree to which the ingroup is included in the self" (p. 586). Degree of ingroup identification is demonstrated by the likelihood of members setting themselves apart or showing solidarity when their identity as group members is threatened (Spears, Doosje, & Ellemers, 1997). High identifiers are more likely to regard the group as homogeneous, feel more committed, and require less individual mobility than low identifiers (Ellemers, Spears, & Doosje, 1997). Along similar lines, Jetten, Spears, and Manstead (2001) found that high identifiers were more willing than low identifiers to protect the group when group identity was threatened. Doosje, Spears, and Ellemers (2002) analyzed the development of ingroup identification with regard to expected changes in intergroup status. They found high identifiers maintained solidarity even if their group faced uncertain prospects (Doosje et al., 2002). In other words, when individuals identify with a group, the group becomes part of their psychological self (Smith, Jackson, & Sparks, 2003), causing individuals to care about the outcome of the group as they would about themselves. The degree to which people identify with a given group has important social consequences (Tyler & Blader, 2001). Ingroup identification increases concern for the group, motivation to follow group norms, and cooperation in social dilemmas. In light of these studies, it is clear that an adolescent's identification with social and political categories is critically important to both the individual and society as a whole, and that social and political identification is a developmental goal related to individual psychological well-being. These studies also imply that identification of young people with their national group should, in the case of heightened political unrest and international intergroup conflict, cause them to care about their country and their national peers.

Our two studies pursued three major goals:

1. In both studies, we first explored to what extent adolescents not directly involved in the Iraqi crisis identify with their particular national ingroup, with Europeans, and as citizens of the world.

2. Our second goal was to explore their fears and predicted changes in the face of war. Although the participating students were not directly targeted by the war, they may have seen the victims of the war and the following terror attacks as more or less close to themselves. It was also conceivable, regardless how likely, that they may have special fears concerning their own person. Additionally, we asked the students about their political attitudes and related them to their reported changes and expectations and degrees of identification. This was done with the intent of providing a better understanding of the complex relationships among the constructs examined. As Tyler and Blader (2001) have pointed out, identity has a strong impact on values and attitudes, and influences one's motivation to voluntary cooperate with the groups one belongs to.

3. In Study 2, our third goal was to compare three European countries which held differing official opinions to the Iraqi crisis: Germany declared itself against military intervention, Switzerland was neutral, and Spain supported and took part in the Iraqi war. We investigated whether students from these countries held different levels of identifications, reporting different attitudes, fears, and expectations.

Study 1 was conducted solely in Germany at the beginning of March 2003 when war in Iraq seemed very likely but had not yet been launched. Study 2 was conducted one year later, during March and April 2004, and data was collected in Germany, Switzerland, and Spain.

STUDY 1

Method

Participants

A sample of 167 German high school students participated in this study. Their mean age was 17.6 years, ranging from 15 to 20 years. More than two thirds of the participants were girls (79%). Nearly half of the students (47.5%) were high school juniors (penultimate year), another 75 students (46.3%) were high school sophomores, and 10 students (6.2%) were seniors.

Procedure

The study was conducted during University Information Days in March 2003 where, over the course of 2 days, high school students are offered on-campus information about subjects that they might like to study after finishing high school. At the beginning of an information session on studying psychology, each student received a questionnaire (described in the following sections). Participation was completely voluntary, instructions were provided both verbally and in writing, and total time required for completion was approximately 20 min.

Measures

Ingroup identification. The single-item pictorial measure, Inclusion of Ingroup in the Self (IIS; see Schubert & Otten, 2002; Tropp & Wright, 2001) was used to assess the degree of identification with an ingroup. It is based on the Inclusion of Others in the Self Scale (Aron, Aron, & Smollan, 1992) and consists of seven Venn diagrams with pairs of circles differing in degree of overlap (Tropp & Wright, 2001). The respondents were asked to select the pair of circles that best represented their extent of identification with the given ingroup. The instrument was translated into German and adapted to include the following groups: Germans, Europeans, Americans, and citizens of the world. Additionally we assumed that individuals usually have a range of different, cross-cutting social identities due to memberships in groups of different personal importance (Jetten et al., 2001). Next to identification with national or political categories, we were interested in a primary social category (Ellemers, Spears, & Doosje, 2002) that students regard as very important to them. Therefore, we asked them to name a group important to them and give their identification with this group. All students received exactly the same questionnaire; each participant rated her or his identification with the Germans, Europeans, Americans, citizens of the world, and a freely chosen group to which one belongs and is important to oneself.

Attitudes towards the current political situation. Separate items were used to assess the attitudes towards the current political situation. The following three items were scored on a 6-point scale ranging from 1 (*strongly disagree*) to 6 (*strongly agree*): (a) "I do not care about politics," (b) "The crisis in Iraq is very important for Germany (the same for: Europe, the world, me personally)," and (c) "I am in favor of leading a war against Iraq."

Expected personal changes in case of war in Iraq.   Additionally, participants were asked, "What personal changes do you expect in case of a war in Iraq?" This exploratory question was answered by a short, written text.

Demographic items.   Respondents were also asked to give their age, gender, and class-year at school.

Results

Identification.   According to Tropp and Wright (2001), scores between 1 and 4 on the IIS were regarded as low-identification responses, and scores between 5 and 7 were considered high-identification responses. The students reported moderate identification with Germans ($M = 3.99$, $SD = 1.56$) and Europeans ($M = 4.06$, $SD = 1.63$), lower identifications with citizens of the world ($M = 3.71$, $SD = 2.00$), and almost no identification with Americans ($M = 2.09$, $SD = 1.43$). No significant differences were found between the identification of these German students with Germans or Europeans ($M = 4.06$, $SD = 1.63$), $t(166) = .51$, $p = .608$ (two-tailed), and Germans and citizens of the world ($M = 3.71$, $SD = 2.00$), $t(163) = 1.57$, $p = .118$ (two-tailed).

Asked about freely-chosen groups of personal importance with which they belonged, almost 20% of the students mentioned friends, more than 10% reported families, and about 5% referenced both groups (see Table 1). Identification with freely-chosen groups ($M = 5.98$, $SD = 1.41$) was significantly higher than identification with Germans ($M = 3.99$, $SD = 1.56$), $t(137) = 11.97$, $p < .01$ (two-tailed).

Attitudes towards the current political situation.   Nearly a quarter (22.4%) of the students reported not caring about politics ($M = 2.46$), yet 11.0% said that they were in favor of leading a war against Iraq ($M = 1.69$). Regarding the importance of the Iraqi crisis, the students postulated high importance for Germany ($M = 4.60$), for Europe ($M = 4.85$), for the world ($M = 5.09$), and for themselves ($M = 4.17$). The items concerning the importance of the Iraqi crisis for Germany, Europe, and the world could be combined into one scale for assessing the global importance of the Iraqi crisis ($\alpha = .88$). Students low in identification with Americans (IIS-responses ranging from 1–4, $n = 148$) also reported a statistically significant lower support for military intervention in Iraq than those students who identified highly with Americans (IIS-responses ranging from 5–7, $n = 14$), $F(1, 160) = 6.96$, $p < .01$. The reported global importance of the Iraqi crisis was negatively correlated with the support for military intervention, $r(158) = .23$, $p < .01$.

TABLE 1
Categories for the Freely-Chosen Group(s)

Categories For the Freely-Chosen Group(s)	Absolute Frequency	Relative Frequency
Family	20	11.98
Friends	33	19.76
Family and friends	8	4.79
Classmates, school, class-year	10	5.99
Students	5	2.99
National group (e.g., "Russians")	8	4.79
Religious group (e.g., "Catholics")	8	4.79
Sports club, association	18	10.78
Women	4	2.40
Europeans	2	1.20
Humans	3	1.80
Geographic places, countries	7	4.19
Teenagers	6	3.59
Others	7	4.19
Missing (no response)	28	16.77
N	167	100

Personal changes or fears expected in case of war.   Categories for the reported personal changes or fears in case of war (reported with a short, written text) were developed by the first author. The answers were then coded by the first author and one blind independent coder. Their agreement within the nine resulting categories reached an average κ of .71. Seventeen students (10.20%) reported global anxiety (e.g., "anxiety"), 12 students (7.20%) talked about specific anxiety (e.g., "fear for friends" and "afraid of terrorist attacks"), 8 students (4.80%) reported changes in global attitudes (e.g., "resignation" and "different attitude towards life"), 19 students (11.40%) expressed changes in specific attitudes (e.g., "mistrusting of politicians"), 7 students (4.%) mentioned changes in behavior ("being more careful"), and 10 students (6%) talked about economic fears (e.g., "rising prices for petrol" and "restricted travel possibilities"). Fifteen students (9%) reported no predicted personal changes and another 9% reported other predicted changes. Forty percent of the students did not respond to the question.

Only one meaningful but slight association between identification and fears and predicted changes was found: identification with Europeans was positively related to changes in global anxiety, $r(167) = .17, p < .05$. Multivariate analyses of variance revealed interesting effects of identification on the reported personal fears and predicted changes: students high in identification with Germans reported more specific anxiety, $F(1, 108) = 5.75, p < .05, \eta^2 = .05$, and fewer changes in behavior, $F(1, 108) = 6.13, p < .05, \eta^2 = .05$. Those students who identified highly with Americans reported less global anxiety, $F(1, 108) = 4.74, p < .05, \eta^2 = .04$, more no changes, $F(1, 108) = 14.46$, $p < .001$, $\eta^2 = .12$, and more changes in global attitudes, $F(1, 108) = 5.35$, $p < .05$, $\eta^2 = .05$.

Regarding possible effects of attitudes on identification, only one weak main effect was found: Students who saw a high global importance of the Iraqi crisis identified less with Germans, $F(1, 112) = 4.1$, $p < .05$, $\eta^2 = .04$. Concerning possible effects of identification on attitudes only two weak main effects were found: Students who identified highly with Europeans reported less support for military intervention in Iraq, $F(1, 99) = 6.96$, $p < .01$, $\eta^2 = .07$, and those who identified highly with their freely-chosen group reported caring less about politics, $F(1,99) = 5.78$, $p < .05$, $\eta^2 = .06$.

No effect was found for age but was found for gender: men identified less with Germans than did women, $F(1, 165) = 4.28$, $p < .05$, $\eta^2 = .03$.

Discussion

Identification.   On average, the German high school students articulate rather low identification scores with their national group. By comparison, they identify much more with their primary groups such as family and friends. The highest degree of any national and political identification is with their nationality, *Germans*, and next-highest with Europeans.

Mullin and Hogg (1998) found that people join or form groups to reduce uncertainty, joining one group rather than another because it is contextually salient for reduction of uncertainty. As young people rely more on relationships with friends, family, sports buddies, and classmates as a source of identification rather than on nationality, we might conclude that primary groups offer more security than more inclusive groups, such as politically defined social entities. We might further speculate that, in times of reduced certainty and security brought on by the threat of war, young people tend to retreat to their private relationships.

Multiple identifications seem to be a way of balancing the need to belong with the need to be different. As stated in the optimal distinctiveness theory (Brewer, 1991; Klandermans, Sabucedo, & Rodriguez, 2004), people are driven not only by the need for distinctiveness but also for inclusiveness and strive to find equilibrium between the two. Within a relatively nonspecific category such as Germans, the students were possibly motivated to achieve greater distinctiveness by identifying with smaller subgroups (e.g., friends, sports club) and perceptually enhancing their distinctiveness by reporting low identification with the broader group, Germans.

We found the rather low degree of identification with Germans interesting and postulate that it might be due to a perception of low group support. McKimmie et al. (2003) contended that lack of support from a salient ingroup can cause attitude changes and reduced levels of identification. Because of the difficult economic and political situation in Germany during and after the debate over military intervention, German students possibly did not feel sufficiently supported by their national ingroup and therefore reduced their degree of identification.

As stated earlier, a further possible reason for low national identification is found in the developmental aspect of identification. In the sense suggested by Hall (2001), identity can be considered a social construct that extends across the life span of human development. Hall argued that the impact of historical events, such as international conflict, on identity development intensifies during one's life span. Because of the cross-sectional character of our study, we can only speculate whether the perception of the Iraqi crisis led to a decrease of national identification or stymied national identification. But, as identification with Germans was related to specific anxieties reported by the participants, it seems appropriate to say that national identification plays a role in the perception and processing of international political tension in young people.

Another explanation for this low ingroup identification is offered by Doosje and Branscombe (2003). Their study pointed out that ingroup identification predicts the perception of a homogeneous outgroup and is linked to internal attributions for negative outgroup behavior. People who identify with their ingroup are relatively likely to perceive the outgroup in negative, stereotypical terms. One could, therefore, argue that the rather low identification with Germans as an ingroup may allow the German students to perceive outgroups in a less stereotypical way and to have a more realistic view regarding possible reasons for outgroup behavior (e.g., the negatively perceived intention of a military intervention in Iraq by the United States and Great Britain).

As reported, the next highest national/political identification score after Germans was with Europe. One reason may be that during the debate over how to manage the Iraqi crisis, Europe had become a salient political category because of the antagonism between the United States and those European states against the war, such as France and Germany (so-called "old Europe").

Students low in identification with Americans also reported statistically lower support for military intervention than students high in identification with Americans. This piques the question of whether low identification with the United States resulted in a rejection of intervention, or whether the rejection led to a critical view of Americans. Answers to this question are beyond the scope of this study.

Attitudes towards the current political situation.   Asked for their attitudes towards the current political situation, most of the German students seemed to care about politics and be against war in Iraq. Only a minority was in favor of military intervention in Iraq. This supports the results of several polls during the prephase of the war, that in most European countries only a minority of the population supported military intervention. Overall, the students regard the Iraqi crisis as carrying great weight, especially for Europe and the world. Interesting is the negative relation between the reported global importance of the Iraqi crisis and the support for military intervention. As this is only a correlational result, one cannot predict if the perceived high importance led to an antiwar attitude or if the reported lower global importance of the Iraqi crisis is, perhaps in terms of dissonance reduction, caused by the stronger support for military intervention in Iraq.

Expected personal changes in case of war.   Nearly half the students did not answer the question concerning personal changes in case of war. We can only speculate on whether the students did not dare explore their feelings towards war, as it would have been too frightening to articulate fears; or the less plausible possibility that they did not expect any changes to their lives in case of war. Other possibilities are that the students just did not know about changes or could not articulate them. The fact that answering this question required a short, written answer could also mean the students simply ignored the question. Nevertheless, the option that students could freely respond without their answers being prejudiced or limited to finite choices proved advantageous in unveiling true feelings. Many of the students who did answer the question reported heightened fears and anxiety. This outcome fits the results of studies investigating the impact of stressful events and terrorist attacks on psychological well being (Silver, Holman, McIntosh, Poulin, & Gil-Rivas, 2002), even when people are not directly targeted (Poilkolainen et al., 1998). The reported changes in attitudes are either of a general nature (e.g., "resignation" and "different attitude towards life") or specific (e.g., "mistrusting of politicians"). The reported changes in behavior can be regarded as realizing positive intentions ("being more careful," "more demonstrations," and "supporting pacifists"). But at the prospect of war, people seem to not only be concerned about their ingroups and related fears but also about probable economic changes such as rising petrol prices and restricted travel.

Concerning the integrated threat theory (Stephan, Diaz-Loving, & Duran, 2000), which suggests four types of threats leading to prejudice toward outgroup members (realistic threats, symbolic threats, intergroup anxiety, and negative stereotypes), the reported fears, anxiety, and predicted economic changes can be regarded as realistic threats, because they refer to physical and material well-being. Integrated threat theory emphasizes the subjectively perceived component within the realistic threats (Stephan & Stephan, 1996). Whether the threat is real or not, the greater the threat an outgroup supposedly poses to the ingroup, the greater the prejudice toward the outgroup. The reported realistic threats in our study are not directly related to a specific outgroup which poses threats. This is probably due to the still vague state of the Iraqi crisis during the time of the survey and might have changed once war broke out and diverse consequences were revealed.

STUDY 2

Study 1 reveals an interesting pattern of identification, attitudes, and expected changes in the face of war. The war in Iraq began on March 20, 2003, and was officially declared over after 5 weeks, followed by an ongoing period of attacks, taking of hostages, and escalating battles in Iraq. One year after the onset of this war, we decided to conduct a second study to find out what had changed after the beginning of war and what new expectations have emerged. The second study followed a similar design to the first one but we decided to take the following two points into account:

1.   Several studies have shown that participants high in public collective self-esteem show more commitment to the ingroup. This relationship seems to be moderated by group identification (e. g., De Cremer, 2001). Smith and Tyler (1997) showed that pride and respect are related to self-esteem and group-oriented behaviors. With such studies in mind, we decided to explore social identification more deeply by including the concept of self-esteem.

2.   We suspected that the moderate degree of identification with Germans and Europeans might be due to very different political positions regarding military intervention in Iraq. Furthermore, low national identification with Germans might be a specific German problem of not feeling free to declare national commitment and identification, due to negative associations with German history—specifically the Holocaust. It might be difficult for German people to distinguish between *patriotism,* which reflects a bias towards ingroup favoritism (Leyens et al., 2003), and *nationalism,* which can carry an additional association with outgroup derogation. We therefore decided to compare identifications of students from various European nationalities in Study 2.

Method

Participants

A sample of 49 Spanish students (18%), 117 Swiss students (43%), and 106 German students (39%) participated in this study. The German students who participated in Study 2 were different from those who participated in Study 1. The participant mean age was 17.9 years (Spanish, 17.8 years; Swiss, 16.9 years; German, 19 years), ranging from 15 to 21 years. More than half (60.3%) of the participants were girls (Spanish, 61.2%; Swiss, 59.2%; German, 61.2%), and all participants were high school students. Participation was completely voluntary, instructions were provided both verbally and in writing, and total time required for completion was approximately 30 min.

Procedure

The study was conducted in high schools in Spain (Salamanca), Switzerland (Bern), and Germany (Goettingen) during March and April 2004. Access to the students was acquired via personal contacts with principals of the high schools. Similar to Study 1, each student received a questionnaire in his or her mother tongue. Because of the low degree of ingroup identification in the German-only Study 1 and possible problematic semantics with the term *Germans*, a pretest was run to collect associations with this term. Nine students completed a free listing (Borgatti, 1999): three of them were asked to make free associations with the term *Germans*; another three students were asked to do likewise with the term *citizens of the FRG (Federal Republic of Germany)*; and the last three students made free associations with the term *inhabitants of Germany*. Results showed very different semantic associations with these terms (see Table 2), confirming our suspicions of semantic problems with the term *German* in Study 1.

Because of the different associations related to the three terms, three distinct versions of the questionnaire were developed. The versions differed only with regard to the use of either *Germans/Spanish/Swiss, citizens of the FRG (Federal Republic of Germany)/Spain/Switzerland*, or *inhabitants of Germany/Spain/Switzerland*. Table 3 shows the distribution of the participants over the nine groups.

TABLE 2
Results of the Freelisting: Major Associations With the Germans,
the Citizens of the FRG, and the Inhabitants of Germany

Term	Associations
Germans	Nazis, world war, Jews, Bavaria, discipline, fight, football, manifold, bright skin
Citizens of the FRG (Federal Republic of Germany)	men, women, elections, tidy, dutiful, reunion, GDR, Europe, Germany, political speech, Bundespräsident
Inhabitants of Germany	citizen, taxpayer, neighbors, registration office, more than 80 million, right to vote, apolitically

TABLE 3
Number of Participants Distributed Over Countries and IIS-Versions

Version of IIS Items Concerning the Own National Group	Location of data collection			
	Germany	Switzerland	Spain	Σ
"Germans"/"Swiss"/"Spanish"	36	41	17	94
"Citizens of Germany [Switzerland, Spain]"	35	37	17	89
"Inhabitants of Germany [Switzerland, Spain]"	35	39	15	89
Σ	106	117	49	272

Note.   IIS = Inclusion of Ingroup in the Self (Tropp & Wright, 2001).

Measures

Ingroup identification.   As in Study 1, the instrument IIS (Tropp & Wright, 2001) was used to assess the degree of identification with the ingroup. The measure was translated into German and Spanish and adapted to include the following group memberships: Germans, Spanish, Swiss, Europeans, Americans, citizens of the world, and a freely-chosen group to which one belongs and is important to oneself.

Collective self-esteem.   The Collective Self-Esteem Scale (Luthanen & Crocker, 1992) was used to measure the collective self-esteem of each participant. This 16-item scale is composed of four subscales, measuring the importance of one's group memberships to one's self-concept (*identity*), feelings of worthiness as a group member (*membership esteem*), personal regard for one's group (*private collective self-esteem*), and assessment of how others evaluate one's social groups (*public collective self-esteem*). Item responses ranged from 1 (*strongly disagree*) to 7 (*strongly agree*). For data collection in Spain, the scales were translated into Spanish by a Spanish native speaker and a Spanish-speaking German psychologist. In Switzerland and Germany, the German version of the Collective Self-Esteem Scale was used (Wagner & Zick, 1993). The reported alpha coefficients ranged from .68 to .80 for the four German subscales.

To focus specifically on membership in nationally defined groups, items were modified according to the nationality in question (e.g., "I am a worthy member of the German nationality"). The adapted subscales show alpha coefficients ranging from .67 to .76.

Attitudes towards the current political situation.   Similar to Study 1, several items were used to obtain the attitudes towards the current political situation in Iraq. The following three items were scored on a 6-point scale ranging from 1 (*strongly disagree*) to 6 (*strongly agree*): (a) "The current situation in Iraq is an important topic for me," (b) "I do not care about politics," and (c) "The crisis in Iraq is very important for... (Germany/Spain/Switzerland, Europe, the world, America, the personally-important group, me)."

Personal changes and expectations.   Similar to Study 1, participants were asked about the personal changes they experienced since the beginning of the Iraqi crisis and about their personal expectations and fears towards the current developments in Iraq. These exploratory questions were answered by a short, written text.

Demographic items.   Participants were also asked to give their age, gender, class-year, and nationality. During the Study 2 survey conducted in Germany, the very last question asked was, "If you think it is problematic being a German—why?" This question was asked to ascertain any subjective reasons for perceived difficulties the German students might have with being German. Almost a third (30.19%, $n = 32$) admitted they had problems for the following reasons: nationality identification problems with special characteristic traits of the Germans (14.2%, $n = 15$), with related problems with history of Germany (10.4%, $n = 11$), with politics of Germany (3.8%, $n = 4$), and with other people's opinion of Germans (1.9%, $n = 2$).

Results

Identification.   The three versions of the questionnaire described in Methods, which differed in use of the terms *Germans/Spanish/Swiss, citizens of the FRG (Federal Republic of Germany)/Spain/Switzerland,* and *inhabitants of Germany/Spain/Switzerland,* were compared regarding possible differences in degree of identification with the respective national ingroup. Results indicated no significant difference between identification with the *Germans/Spanish/Swiss* ($M = 4.30$, $SD = 1.59$), *citizens of the FRG (Federal Republic of Germany)/Spain/Switzerland* ($M = 4.20$, $SD = 1.55$), and *inhabitants of Germany/Spain/Switzerland* ($M = 4.30$, $SD = 1.34$), $F(2, 266) = 0.15$, $p = .87$. There were also no significant differences within the German sample, $F(2, 103) = 0.21$, $p = .81$, Swiss sample, $F(2, 111) = 0.14$, $p = .87$, and Spanish sample, $F(2, 46) = 0.06$, $p = .97$). We therefore do not distinguish the three versions in further analyses.

Figure 1 shows results of identifications with national groups. The German students ($M = 3.99$, $SD = 1.46$) and Swiss students ($M = 4.21$, $SD = 1.43$) identified moderately with their respective national category, whereas the Spanish students ($M = 5.00$, $SD = 1.51$) identified significantly higher, $F(2, 266) = 8.21$, $p < .01$, $\eta^2 = .06$, with their nationality.

Results showed no significant differences between the German, Swiss, and Spanish student identification with Europeans, $F(2, 264) = 0.23$, $p = .79$, citizens of the world, $F(2, 264) = 1.93$, $p = .15$, and Americans, $F(2, 264) = 1.22$, $p = .27$. There was also no difference within the three samples between identification with own national group ($M = 4.27$, $SD = 1.49$) and Europeans ($M = 4.13$, $SD = 1.50$), $t(268) = 1.52$, $p = .13$ (two-tailed), but a lower identification was shown with citizens of the world ($M = 3.60$, $SD = 1.78$), $t(266) = 5.12$, $p < .01$ (two-tailed), and an even lower identification with Americans ($M = 2.27$, $SD = 1,52$), $t(268) = 16.60$, $p < .01$ (two-tailed).

Regarding the freely chosen groups of personal importance with which one belongs, 38.6% of the students mentioned families, 21.32% reported friends, and 6.62% referenced both. As in Study 1, identification with freely-chosen groups ($M = 5.93$, $SD = 1.26$) was significantly higher than with their national group ($M = 4.27$, $SD = 1.49$), $t(266) = 15.2$, $p < .01$ (two-tailed).

Collective self-esteem.   An adapted version of the Collective Self-Esteem Scale (Luthanen & Crocker, 1992) was used to assess the collective self-esteem of

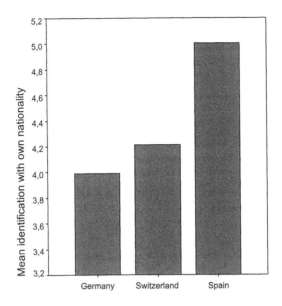

FIGURE 1   Mean identification of German, Swiss, and Spanish students with their nationality. The vertical axis does not start with zero.

the three nationalities and for each nationality. The identity subscale was further adapted for the freely-chosen group.

Results showed moderate national collective self-esteem ($M = 4.52$, $SD = 0.71$) and negligible differences between the German ($M = 4.47$, $SD = 0.76$), Swiss ($M = 4.54$, $SD = 0.65$), and Spanish students ($M = 4.54$, $SD = 0.73$), $F(2, 262) = 0.39$, $p = .68$. National collective self-esteem and the identification with their national group revealed high association, $r(269) = .44$, $p < .01$. Those students who identified highly with own national group reported higher national collective self-esteem, $F(1, 245) = 20.77$, $p < .001$, $\eta^2 = .08$, and those who identified highly with citizens of the world reported less national collective self-esteem, $F(1, 245) = 8,90$, $p < .01$, $\eta^2 = .04$.

Attitudes towards the current political situation.   A   large   majority (78.7%) regarded the Iraqi crisis as a personally important topic. The German ($M = 4.68$, $SD = 1.16$) and Spanish students ($M = 4.61$, $SD = 1.24$) regarded it equally personally important and the Swiss students ($M = 4.21$, $SD = 1.27$) regarded it as less personally important, $F(2, 269) = 4.63$, $p < .05$, $\eta^2 = .03$, than did the other two groups. Concerning the postulated importance of the Iraqi crisis to their own country, the Spanish students ($M = 5.16$, $SD = 1.01$) perceived it as more important than the German students ($M = 4.30$, $SD = 1.00$) and the German students postulated higher national importance than the Swiss students ($M = 3.17$, $SD = 1.20$), $F(2, 267) = 64.90$, $p < .01$, $\eta^2 = .33$. Overall, the highest importance of the Iraqi crisis was postulated for the United States ($M = 5.47$, $SD = 0.99$), followed by the world ($M = 5.24$, $SD = 0.95$), $t(271) = 3.11$, $p < .01$ (two-tailed), and Europe ($M = 4.90$, $SD = 0.99$), $t(271) = 6.15$, $p < .01$ (two-tailed). Those students who identified with citizens of the world reported a higher personal importance of the Iraqi crisis, $F(1, 202) = 8.38$, $p < .01$, $\eta^2 = .03$.

An even larger majority (79.1%) reported caring about politics. The German students cared the most ($M = 1.88$, SD 1.17), followed by the Swiss students ($M = 2.26$, $SD = 1.33$). The Spanish students cared the least of the three nationalities ($M = 3.24$, $SD = 1.60$), $F(2, 269) = 17.92$, $p < .01$, $\eta^2 = .12$. Multivariate analysis revealed interesting results: students who identified highly with citizens of the world reported caring more about politics, $F(1, 202) = 4.85$, $p < .05$, $\eta^2 = .03$, but those who identified highly with own national group or with Americans reported caring less about politics, $F(1, 202) = 4.75$, $p < .05$, $\eta^2 = .02$, and $F(1, 202) = 7.59$, $p < .01$, $\eta^2 = .04$. No further relations between identification and attitudes were found.

Personal changes and fears in face of the Iraqi crisis.   Similar to Study 1, categories for reported personal changes and fears in case of war (reported with a short, written text) were developed by the first author. The answers were then coded by the first author and one blind independent coder. Their agreement (Cohen's κ) within the eight resulting categories for *personal changes since the beginning of the Iraqi crisis* ranged from .74 to .99, except for the category *more concern and worries* ($\kappa = .61$), and within the eleven resulting categories for *fears in face of the current situation in Iraq* ($\kappa = .77$ to .91), except for *other fears* ($\kappa = .59$). Figures 2 and 3 illustrate resulting categories and percentage of frequencies.

As shown in Figures 2 and 3, the students from the three countries differed in reported changes and fears. Regarding changes since the beginning of the Iraqi crisis, the Spanish reported more concern and worries than the Swiss and German students, $F(2, 269) = 6.16$, $p < .01$, $\eta^2 = .04$. The Swiss students showed more consciousness concerning political conflict than the Spanish students, $F(2, 269) = 3.63$, $p < .05$, $\eta^2 = .03$, and less anxiety than the German and Spanish students, $F(2, 269) = 4.26$, $p < .01$, $\eta^2 = .03$.

Regarding reported fears and expectations in face of the current situation in Iraq, the German students feared rising terror more than the Swiss and Spanish students, $F(2, 269) = 21.62$, $p < .001$, $\eta^2 = .14$. Also, the German and Swiss students reported more worries concerning the difficult and powerful position of the USA than the Spanish students, $F(2, 269) = 6.22$, $p < .01$, $\eta^2 = .04$. No further significant differences were found.

Regarding the relation between reported changes and fears and group identifications, only a few effects could be found: students who identified highly with their national group were more apt to report no worries, $F(1, 251) = 6.02$ $p < .05$,

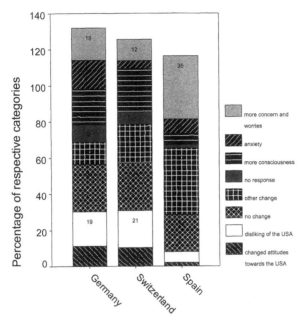

FIGURE 2 Percentage of categories of the reported personal changes since beginning of Iraqi crisis. Numbers do not sum up to 100%. Multiple answers are possible.

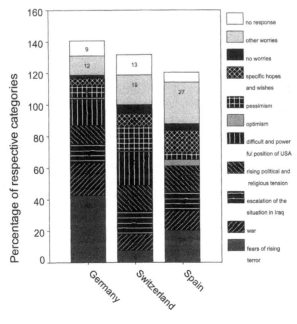

FIGURE 3 Percentage of categories of the reported personal fears and expectations in face of current Iraqi situations. Numbers do not sum up to 100%. Multiple answers are possible.

$\eta^2 = .02$. Also, those who identified highly with Europeans reported more fear of escalation of the situation in Iraq, $F(1, 251) = 4.90$, $p < .05$, $\eta^2 = .02$. Students high in identification with citizens of the world reported less fear of rising terror, $F(1, 251) = 5.02$, $p < .05$, $\eta^2 = .02$. And interestingly, students high in identification with Americans reported fewer worries concerning the difficult and powerful situation of the United States, $F(1, 251) = 5.59$, $p < .05$, $\eta^2 = .02$.

Regarding the relation between reported changes and fears and the political attitudes previously noted, again only a few effects could be found. Students who reported caring about politics reported more consciousness concerning political conflict, $F(1, 263) = 6.43$, $p < .05$, $\eta^2 = .02$, and were more likely to fear rising political and religious tension, $F(1, 263) = 4.89$, $p < .05$, $\eta^2 = .02$. Those who saw the Iraqi crisis as personally important were less apt to report no changes, $F(1, 263) = 6.26$, $p < .05$, $\eta^2 = .02$. No effects for age and gender were found.

Discussion

Identification and collective self-esteem. As in Study 1, the German, as well as the Swiss, students articulate rather low identification with their respective nationalities. This contrasts sharply with the Spanish students, who report identifying highly with their nationality. Similar to Study 1, the nation does not seem to be a valuable source of identification to young German and Swiss people, who do not differ in their national identification compared to their identification as Europeans. For Study 2, Europe had probably become a more salient group for two reasons: the European controversy about military intervention in Iraq, and the enlargement of the European Union in May 2004. We can only speculate about reasons for higher national identification among the Spanish students—specifically the March 2004 terrorist attack in Madrid. This tragedy could very well account for being Spanish as gaining salience, high identification with the ingroup serving as a means of reducing fear and insecurity among the Spanish students.

In spite of their differences in national identification, the German, Swiss, and Spanish students surveyed do not differ in their moderate collective national self-esteem, their identification as Europeans, low identification as citizens of the world, and even less identification with Americans. The latter result corresponds with the reported negative evaluation of American policies towards Iraq. There seems to have developed a great gap between the European student political attitude and their perception of American politics.

Similar to Study 1, students identify much more with their primary groups, such as family and friends, than they do with their national group. Corresponding with the moderate national identification of German and Swiss students, they show only moderate levels of national collective self-esteem—the general tendency to evaluate one's social identity concerning one's own national group positively. The national category does not seem to serve as a very important source of identification, except for those students highly identified with their nation—they seem to value their national group as a basis for social identity. Although the Spanish students identify relatively highly with their nation, the national collective self-esteem of Spanish students does not differ from those of the German and Swiss students. It is interesting that a higher identification with citizens of the world predicted lower national collective self-esteem, perhaps suggesting that for those students, a superordinate group is more important for their social identity.

About one third of the German students in Study 2 admit to having problems with their nationality and mainly attribute them to characteristic traits of Germans and German history. As suspected, there seems to be a problem specific to Germans not feeling free to declare themselves committed to their nationality. Even when the term *Germans* is replaced with terms such as *inhabitants of the FRG*, which are less associated with historically political connotations, it does not lead to higher levels of identification with German nationality.

Attitudes towards the current political situation.   Asked about attitudes towards the current political situation in Iraq, most of the students reported caring about politics. The German students care to the highest degree, followed by the Swiss and then by the Spanish students. Overall, the students regard the Iraqi crisis as carrying great weight, especially for the world and for the United States of America. Again, the role of identification with certain groups, especially citizens of the world, is interesting. The students high in identification with the latter seem to care more about politics and report higher personal importance of the Iraqi crisis. Obviously, the category *citizens of the world* plays a crucial role regarding political attitudes.

Personal changes and fears in face of the Iraq crisis.   In Study 2, fears, sorrows, and changing attitudes have become more concrete. Fears concerning the current situation now consist mainly of fear of war and terror, rising international tension, and a worsening situation in Iraq. Economic changes play almost no role. In terms of integrated threat theory (Stephan et al., 2000), along with realistic threats (e.g., fear of war and of terror), there is also mention of symbolic threats such as group differences in morals, values, and beliefs; and fear of rising political and religious tension in the world. Furthermore, the sources of the fears and worries have became more concrete, specifically fear of escalation of the situation in Iraq, as well as changed attitudes toward, and even dislike of, the USA.

Social identification in young people is complicated. Students high in identification with *Americans* reported fewer worries concerning the difficult and powerful situation of the USA. Students who identified highly with citizens of the world reported less fear of rising terror; and those high in identification with their own national group reported fewer worries. This suggests that identification

with these categories, their perceived personally relevant or irrelevant characteristics, as well as the degree of perceived security and support these groups provide, has an impact on a young person's perception of fear and anxiety. Further
research should examine this relationship, especially the apparently important
category of citizens of the world.

The differences in the reported changes and fears among the three countries are
most interesting. The Spanish students reported more concern and worries since
the beginning of the Iraqi crisis than those reported by the German and Swiss students. This difference could be the consequence of several factors. The Spanish
government supported a military intervention in Iraq, leading to massive demonstrations throughout the Spanish nation. In addition, the March 2004 Madrid terror
attacks undoubtedly led to rising concern and played a role internally and exter-
nally in relation to Spain's position in the Iraqi war.

The Swiss students reported less anxiety. This could be explained by the rather
neutral position Switzerland traditionally holds in political conflicts, as well as in
the current Iraqi crisis. Some Swiss students wrote about how they came to appreciate their living in Switzerland as a somewhat safe place.

The Swiss and German students reported more worries than the Spanish students concerning the difficult and powerful situation of the United States. This
may be an outcome of the fact that the Spanish political position in dealing with the
conflict in Iraq was more closely aligned with the United States position than those
of Germany and Switzerland.

CONCLUSION

Given the war in Iraq and its everyday presence in the mass media, our two studies
pursued three goals. First, we explored in both studies to what extent adolescents
who were not directly involved in the Iraqi crisis identified with their own nation,
with Europeans, and as citizens of the world. Our second goal was to explore their
fears and predicted changes in the face of war. Although the participating students
were not directly targeted by the war, it was highly likely that they had seen victims
of the war in the media and perceived the following terror attacks as more or less
close to themselves. Additionally, we asked the students about their current political attitudes and related them to their reported changes and expectations and degrees of identification. In Study 2, our third goal was to compare three European
countries that held differing official positions with respect to the Iraqi crisis. We investigated whether students from Germany, Switzerland, and Spain held different
levels and types of identifications and reported different attitudes, fears, and expectations.

We found that students identify with their national group to a rather low degree.
This holds true for the German samples of both studies and the Swiss sample of

Study 2. Low national identity is even truer for German students because for at least 20 %, being German seems to be precarious. The results from the German subsample showed that it is typically a German problem related to the history of the Third Reich and the Holocaust, and we therefore did not ask the Swiss and Spanish students this question concerning problems associated with their nationality. As the lack of identification differences between German and Swiss compared to identification as European shows, European seems to be a category which can be used for identity purposes, especially for German and Swiss students.

The Spanish students are an exception because they identify highly with their nation. In Spain, extreme events, such as the terrorist bomb attacks in Madrid, happening during data collection probably led people to retreat to their identification with nationality to reduce uncertainty and manage personal and collective fears. Nevertheless, it is fair to say that nationality is not so important for young people. Identification occurs on a more private level with family and friends, and the nation does not seem to be such a useful source of identification.

It is also fair to say that young people are, in fact, afraid of war and terrorist attacks and the threat of international conflict. We found that approximately 20% of the students reported having changed their attitude towards the United States of America for the worse, and see it as deeply involved in the conflict. Those with a critical view of U.S. politics did not identify with the group *Americans*. This can be taken as a cue for an increasingly critical view of American international politics that young people are developing as they process mass media information and communicate with their primary groups.

In sum, we have come to realize that high school students in Europe are well aware of the context and consequences of international conflict, and that they are quite worried about the consequences of war. We consider this an important result because it shows that national or supranational identification (with Europe or the United States) may be a sensible indicator for the cognitive and emotional aspects of political attitudes in view of threatening events such as war and international conflict. Young people have the possibility of gaining security and social identity via groups below the scope of nationality by identifying with primary groups such as familiy and friends. Nevertheless, their opinions, as well as their everyday feelings and worries in times of war, are influenced by the specific historical and present political situation of their home country. They seem to take into account the relative safety (Switzerland), the precarious political history (Germany), and the actual situation (Spain) in their country in a sophisticated way. To have such a timely and informed perspective of the conditions of national identity seems important to us, because a certain degree of identification with the social category of nation is needed to engage in collective action on a national level. This is especially true regarding identification with Europe as a social category to politically act on this level with sufficient support of citizens in Europe.

As a last word about the methodological limitations of Study 2, we must admit that the cross-sectional nature of our investigation prevented us from examining processes and changes in the identity over time. Following the same students over several points of measurement would have revealed more information and a richer picture of the interaction of social identification and political attitudes.

ACKNOWLEDGEMENT

We offer our thanks to the six high schools in Goettingen, Bern, and Salamanca, for their cooperation. We thank Eva Biermeyer, Andreas Hegenbart, Juliane Hinkel, Melanie Jäger, Cornelia Schnur, and Christine John for their assistance in data collection and coding. Thanks are also due to the anonymous reviewers and Richard V. Wagner for their helpful comments on an earlier version of this article. As a final note, we thank our proofreader, Margarita Neff-Heinrich.

BIOGRAPHICAL NOTES

Michaela Kolbe, born in 1977, studied psychology at the Universities of Halle and Göttingen. Since 2003, she has been a research and teaching associate in the Department of Social Psychology and Communication Studies at the Georg-August-University of Göttingen. Her research interests lie in the field of inter– and intragroup processes, especially communication and coordination.

Margarete Boos, born in 1954, studied mathematics and sociology. She received her PhD in sociology from the University of Bonn in 1983, and worked as assistant and associate professor in the Department of Psychology at the University of Konstanz. Since 1995, she has been Professor of Social and Economic Psychology at the University of Göttingen. Her research interests focus on small group research, methods for interaction and communication analysis, computer-mediated communication, and the psychology of brands (e.g. cognitive representation of brand-names).

Andrea Gurtner, born in 1960, is a senior research fellow in the Department of Applied Psychology at the University of Neuchâtel, Switzerland. She received her PhD in psychology from the University of Bern, Switzerland. Her current research interests include reflexivity, communication and coordination processes in teams, and the development of shared mental models.

REFERENCES

Aron, A., Aron, E. N., & Smollan, D. (1992). Inclusion of others in the self scale and the structure of interpersonal closeness. *Journal of Personality and Social Psychology, 63*, 565–612.

Borgatti, S. P. (1999). Elicitation techniques for cultural domain analysis. In J. J. Schensul & M. D. LeCompte (Eds.), *The ethnographic toolkit* (pp. 115–151). Walnut Creek, CA: AltaMira.

Brewer, M. B. (1991). The social self: On being the same and different at the same time. *Personality and Social Psychology Bulletin, 17*, 475–482.

De Cremer, D. (2001). Relations of self-esteem concerns, group identification, and self-stereotyping to in-group favoritism. *Journal of Social Psychology, 141*, 389–400.

Doosje, B., & Branscombe, N. R. (2003). Attributions for the negative historical actions of a group. *European Journal of Social Psychology, 33*, 235–248.

Doosje, B., Spears, R., & Ellemers, N. (2002). Social identity as both cause and effect: The development of group identification in response to anticipated and actual changes in the intergroup status hierarchy. *British Journal of Social Psychology, 41*, 57–76.

Elbedour, S. (1998). Youth in crisis: The well-being of Middle Eastern youth and adolescents during war and peace. *Journal of Youth and Adolescence, 27*, 539–556.

Ellemers, N., Spears, R., & Doosje, B. (1997). Sticking together of falling apart: In-group identification as a psychological determinant of group commitment versus individual mobility. *Journal of Personality and Social Psychology, 72*, 617–626.

Ellemers, N., Spears, R., & Doosje, B. (2002). Self and social identity. *Annual Review of Psychology, 53*, 161–186.

Erikson, E. H. (1950). *Childhood and society.* New York: Norton.

Erikson, E. H. (1968). *Identity: Youth and crisis.* New York: Norton.

Hall, R. E. (2001). Identity development across the lifespan: A biracial model. *Social Science Journal, 38*, 119–123.

Jackson, J. W. (2002). Intergroup attitudes as a function of different dimensions of group identification and perceived intergroup conflict. *Self and Identity, 1*, 11–33.

Jetten, J., Spears, R., & Manstead, A. S. R. (2001). Similarity as a source of differentiation: The role of group identification. *European Journal of Social Psychology, 31*, 621–640.

Kashima, E. S., Kashima, Y., & Hardie, E. A. (2000). Self-typicality and group identification: Evidence for their separateness. *Group Processes and Intergroup Relations, 3*, 97–110.

Klandermans, B., Sabucedo, J. M., & Rodriguez, M. (2004). Inclusiveness of identification among farmers in The Netherlands and Galicia (Spain). *European Journal of Social Psychology, 34*, 279–295.

Leyens, J.-P., Cortes, B., Demoulin, S., Dovidio, J. F., Fiske, S. T., Gaunt, R., et al. (2003). Emotional prejudice, essentialism, and nationalism. The 2002 Tajfel lecture. *European Journal of Social Psychology, 33*, 703–715.

Luthanen, R., & Crocker, J. (1992). A collective self-esteem scale: Self-evaluations of one's social identity. *Personality and Social Psychology Bulletin, 18*, 302–318.

Makros, J., & McCabe, M. P. (2001). Relationships between identity and self-representations during adolescence. *Journal of Youth and Adolescence, 30*, 623–639.

Marcia, J. E. (1980). Identity in adolescence. In J. Adelson (Ed.), *Handbook of adolescent psychology* (pp. 159–187). Brisbane, New York: Wiley.

Martinez, R. O., & Dukes, R. L. (1997). The effect of ethnic identity, ethnicity, and gender on adolescent well-being. *Journal of Youth and Adolescence, 26*, 503–516.

McKimmie, B. M., Terry, D. J., Hogg, M. A., Manstead, A. S. R., Spears, R., & Doosje, B. (2003). I'm a hypocrite, but so is everyone else: Group support and the reduction of cognitive dissonance. *Group Dynamics, 7*, 214–224.

Mullin, B.-A., & Hogg, M. A. (1998). Dimensions of subjective uncertainty in social identification and minimal intergroup discrimination. *British Journal of Social Psychology, 37*, 345–365.

Poilkolainen, K., Kanerva, R., & Lönnqvist, J. (1998). Increasing fear of nuclear war among adolescents before the outbreak of the Persian Gulf War. *Nordic Journal of Psychiatry, 52*, 197–202.

Poole, M. S., Hollingshead, A. B., McGrath, J. E., Moreland, R. L., & Rohrbaugh, J. (2004). Interdisciplinary perspectives on small groups. *Small Group Research, 35*, 3–16.

Ramsay, A. (2002). The problem of Iraq. *Contemporary Review, 281*, 193–199.

Schubert, T. W., & Otten, S. (2002). Overlap of self, ingroup, and outgroup: Pictorial measures of self-categorization. *Self and Identity, 1*, 353–376.

Schwartz, S. J., & Montgomery, M. J. (2002). Similarities or differences in identity development? The impact of acculturation and gender on identity process and outcome. *Journal of Youth and Adolescence, 31*, 359–372.

Silver, R. C., Holman, E. A., McIntosh, D. N., Poulin, M., & Gil-Rivas, V. (2002). Nationwide longitudinal study of psychological responses to September 11. *Journal of the American Medical Association, 288*, 1235–1244.

Smith, E. R., Jackson, J. W., & Sparks, C. W. (2003). Effects of inequality and reasons for inequality on group identification and cooperation in social dilemmas. *Group Processes and Intergroup Relations, 6*, 201–220.

Smith, H. J., & Tyler, T. R. (1997). Choosing the right pond: The impact of group membership on self esteem and group-orientated behavior. *Journal of Experimental Social Psychology, 33*, 146–170.

Spears, R., Doosje, B., & Ellemers, N. (1997). Self-stereotyping in the face of threats to group status and distinctiveness: The role of group identification. *Personality and Social Psychology Bulletin, 23*, 538–553.

Stephan, W. G., Diaz-Loving, R., & Duran, A. (2000). Integrated threat theory and intercultural attitudes. *Journal of Cross-Cultural Psychology, 31*, 240–249.

Stephan, W. G., & Stephan, C. W. (1996). Predicting prejudice. *International Journal of Intercultural Relations, 20*, 409–426.

Stringer, M., Cornish, I. M., & Denver, S. (2000). The transition to peace and young people's perceptions of locations in Northern Ireland. *Peace and Conflict: Journal of Peace Psychology, 6*, 57–66.

Tajfel, H., & Turner, J. C. (1986). The social identity theory of intergroup behavior. In S. Worchel & W. G. Austin (Eds.), *Psychology of intergroup relations* (2nd ed., pp. 7–24). Chicago: Nelson-Hall.

Tropp, L. R., & Wright, S. C. (1999). Ingroup identification and relative deprivation: An examination across multiple social comparisons. *European Journal of Social Psychology, 29*, 707–724.

Tropp, L. R., & Wright, S. C. (2001). Ingroup identification as the inclusion of ingroup in the self. *Personality and Social Psychology Bulletin, 27*, 585–600.

Turner, J. C. (1985). Social categorization and the self-concept: A social cognitive theory of group behavior. In E. J. Lawler (Ed.), *Advances in group processes* (Vol. 2, pp. 77–121). Greenwich, CT: JAI Press.

Turner, J. C., Sydney, N. S. W., Hogg, M. A., Oakes, P.-J., Reicher, S. D., & Wetherell, M. S. (1987). *Rediscovering the social group: A self-categorization theory.* Cambridge, MA: Blackwell.

Tyler, T. R., & Blader, S. L. (2001). Identity and cooperative behavior in groups. *Group Processes and Intergroup Relations, 4*, 207–226.

Wagner, H., & Zick, A. (1993). Selbstdefinitionen und Intergruppenbeziehungen: Der Social Identity Approach [Self definition and intergroup relations: The social identity approach.]. In E. Pörzgen & E. H. Witte (Eds.), *Selbstkonzept und Identität. Beiträge des 8. Hamburger Symposiums zur Methodologie der Sozialpsychologie* [*Self concept and identity: Contributions to the 8th Symposium on Methodology in Social Psychology*] (pp. 109–129). Braunschweig, Germany: Braunschweiger Studien.

PEACE AND CONFLICT: JOURNAL OF PEACE PSYCHOLOGY, *11*(3), 337–354

Once a Peacenik—Always a Peacenik? Results From a German Six-Wave, Twenty-Year Longitudinal Study

Klaus Boehnke
International University Bremen

Mandy Boehnke
University of Bremen

This article documents results of an ongoing 20-year, 6-wave longitudinal study of 201 German peace movement sympathizers, first surveyed in 1985 at an average age of 14½. The aim of the part of the study reported in this article is to predict current political involvement on the grounds of knowledge about earlier cognitive, emotional, and conative political involvement. Regression analyses show that it is not so much early engagement in political activities, like going to demonstrations, that let's one predict middle adulthood political mobilization but early cognitive and emotional involvement with politics, like being alarmed about ongoing stressful macrosocial conditions. With regard to cognitive involvement, factual knowledge about politics plays a more important role than early self-actualization values in the Inglehartian sense do. Altogether, approximately 12% of the variance in current political involvement of individuals in their mid-30s can be explained on the grounds of information about life circumstances and attitudes in adolescence.

In the early 1980s, the Cold War between the West and the real socialist bloc came to another, its final, peak. The Soviet Union had deployed so-called SS 20 missiles on the soil of East Germany, the then German Democratic Republic, as a reaction to what the Warsaw Agreement states saw as an arms build-up of the West. The West reacted by deploying Pershings and Cruise Missiles, among others, on the soil of the Federal Republic of Germany, and called this "re-armament." The peace

---

Correspondence should be sent to Klaus Boehnke, Professor of Social Science Methodology, International University Bremen, Campus Ring 1, D–28759–Bremen, Germany. E-mail: K.Boehnke@ iu-bremen.de

movement fiercely opposed these armament measures in the West and even in some grassroots activities in the East. There were demonstrations in Bonn, then the capital of Germany, that saw over 1 million participants. Psychologists and physicians wondered whether the threat of nuclear war that emanated from this political and military deadlock would have an affect on the mental health, particularly of children and adolescents.

Research on this topic published in the 1980s often took an alarmist position (e.g., Beardslee, & Mack, 1983), expecting and sometimes reporting considerable mental health effects of *macrosocial stress*, a term coined by the first author in articles in *Political Psychology* and in the *Psychiatry Digest* (Boehnke, Macpherson, Meador, & Petri, 1989; Boehnke, Fromberg, & Macpherson, 1992). Early studies showed that children and adolescents were very worried by the prospect of a nuclear war all around the world, that is, in North America (Sommers, Goldberg, Levinson, Ross, & LaCombe, 1985), in Eastern Europe (Wasilewski, 1989), in the then so-called neutral countries (Solantaus, Rimpelä, & Taipale, 1984), as well as the developing world (Ardila, 1986). It did, however, quickly become clear that a mechanistic medical stress model that assumed a linear relation between great worries and poor mental health could not be corroborated. On the contrary, several studies showed that those children and adolescents who worried most were the ones with the best mental health status (Meyer-Probst, Teichmann, & Kleinpeter, 1989; Newcomb, 1986, 1988). This finding led to a paradigmatic shift in the study of macrosocial stress. The cognitive-phenomenological stress model (Lazarus & Folkman, 1984) became more prominent in explaining the mental health effects of fear of nuclear war and related worries. Seemingly only mentally sufficiently healthy children and adolescents had sufficient cognitive and emotional capacities to worry about something as remote to their everyday lives as missile deployment.

When the smoke of the Cold War had eventually vanished, it became more and more clear that consequences of macrosocial stress would lie not so much in the field of mental health but in the field of political participation. Peace movement activities against the deployment of US weaponry on West German soil had been unsuccessful: Pershings and Cruise Missiles were deployed in 1983, following a consenting decision of the West German parliament, the *Bundestag*. Clearly, this was a frustrating experience for peace activists, many of whom were in their adolescent years at the time. The nuclear power catastrophe at Chernobyl in 1986 added to the frustration of the same cohort, as, once again, major public protests had no immediate political consequences. The nuclear power policy of the German government remained virtually unchanged for yet another decade.

In the early 1990s, young people in Germany had other types of macrosocial stress on their minds. They had to cope with the rapid social change brought about by German unification and processes of societal transformation in the years that followed. This, being coupled with noticeable signs of economic crisis in Germany, turned many young people away from political activism. Political alienation or apathy (in German, *Politikverdrossenheit*) became a prominent topic in public discourse. Participation rates in elections dropped substantially from over 91% in (West German) federal elections in 1972 to now 79%, with participation rates in elections to the European parliament as low as 45% in 2004 (Schmitt, 2005). Membership rates in political organizations (parties, unions, etc.) dropped sharply (Gaiser, de Rijke, & Wächter, 2003; Mair & van Biezen, 2001) and were not fully made up by increases in the membership of civil society organizations, like nongovernmental organizations and citizen action groups.

This societal trend puts forward the question how political activism of West German youngsters during the peace movement years in the 1980s is related to current political interest and activism of individuals who had, in large quantities, taken part in such political activities. This article will offer empirical evidence on this question from a longitudinal survey study, which the first author started in 1985, together with three colleagues from the International Physicians for the Prevention of Nuclear War (IPPNW), Nobel Peace Prize recipient of 1985.

Before we come to this study, however, we briefly review the existing literature on determinants of political participation, with focus on Germany. Taking a more general look at social science studies of political participation makes it evident that determinants of political engagement tend to be context-specific, that is, that they often pertain to the specific cultural context of a particular country (Taru, 2003). Reviewing the German literature, it becomes evident that both political psychology and political sociology have only very recently returned to the topic of political participation, after having kept silent for some 15 years, since Klingemann and Kaase (1981) published their book on political psychology. Meanwhile, however, a handbook, *Youth and Politics* (Palentien, & Hurrelmann, 1998), as well as an edited volume on *The Politicization of the Human Being* (Claussen & Geissler, 1996) have appeared. Numerous studies from a special research program by the Deutsche Forschungsgemeinschaft, the German National Science Foundation, on *Childhood and Adolescence in Germany before and after Unification* as well as follow-up studies to that program have dealt with the topic of political socialization and participation (Oswald, 1998). Many of these studies, however, are not longitudinal in their scope.

In a review article, Reinders (2003) reported evidence from five major German longitudinal studies on intraindividual change in political attitudes in the adolescent years. Only two of the reported studies, however, included information on political participation, namely studies by Oswald (1999, Oswald & Schmid, 1998) and Krampen (1991, 2000).

Summarizing evidence from these studies, and drawing on a recent state-of-the-art report by Gaiser, de Rijke, and Wächter (2003), one can highlight the following findings of German research on political participation of youth: The best predictor of political participation is what Inglehart, as early as 1977, called cognitive mobilization. How empirical research is to operationalize cognitive mobilization remains, however, somewhat imprecise. Quite frequently, value orientation measures have been suggested as measures *par excellence* of cognitive mobilization (Gille, Krüger, de Rijke, & Willems, 1998; Inglehart, 1977). Within Inglehart's conceptual framework, this means that self-actualization values, or what he earlier called postmaterialist values, are the best predictors of political interest and participation. Hoffmann-Lange (1998) and Gabriel (1986, 1997) understood cognitive mobilization more in the sense of an active cognitive involvement in political on-goings, a notion closely resembling ideas brought forward by Krampen (2000). Boehnke, Fuß, and Rupf (2001) called attention to the mobilizing role of macrosocial worries. Krampen (2000) emphasized that mere political knowledge may also serve as a proxy for cognitive mobilization.

Apart from these psychological determinants of political participation, certain sociodemographic variables also play a role in the prediction of political participation. Girls and women tend to have less interest in participating in politics than do boys and men. Political interest, and to some degree participation, increases with age in youth and young adulthood. The higher a person's formal educational attainment, the stronger his or her political interest and participation.

For high degrees of involvement in politics, it is obviously decisive that young people experience politics as being something important early in their lives. The more cognitive mobilization they experience vis-a-vis the political sphere, the more prone they are to become active in that sphere. Even though concrete political engagement is often only undertaken in adulthood, the basis for individuals to become a *zoon politicon*, a political animal, is laid much earlier, namely in early to middle adolescence at the latest.

Without formulating specific hypotheses, in the remainder of this text we want to test whether the importance of what Inglehart (1977) called cognitive mobilization has a long term impact on individual political participation and not only the cross-sectional impact that has repeatedly been shown. In detail, stability and change in political participation and interest between the ages of 14 and 32 are documented. As briefly mentioned, this will be done by reporting data from a 6-wave longitudinal study, started in 1985, in West Germany.

METHODS

Sample

In 1985, at a time when the Cold War between the Soviet Bloc and NATO escalated for one final time, a research team in West Berlin started a research project titled "Life under Nuclear Threat," with support from the German branch and the Boston head office of the IPPNW. The original goal of the project was to document the prevalence of existential anxieties among Berlin children and adolescents, and the impact such anxieties have on their mental health. This goal quickly had to be abandoned, as the conservative decision makers of the city at that time rejected the proposal of conducting a representative study in schools, as (quoted from a letter by the then-minister for educational affairs in Berlin) "not in the interest of the educational intentions of Berlin." The study quickly became part of the political controversies around the awarding of the Nobel Peace Prize to IPPNW. Peter Hofstätter (1985), nestor of German Military Psychology, wrote a column in the conservative daily *Die Welt* under the title "Frightening Children," accompanied by a cartoon labeled "Doctor Games," in which an IPPNW doctor threatens a child in a baby carriage with an injection needle that has "No future" written on it. Nevertheless, the group succeeded in conducting a large study on the topic of children's and adolescents' existential anxieties, despite having to give up the representativeness aim.

The initial sample was obtained through controlled snowballing in Summer, 1985. Through advertisements in pertinent publication outlets and personal contacts of the researchers, individuals who worked with children were approached as to whether they would be willing to cooperate with the research team. These cooperation partners were requested to distribute the four-page questionnaire that the team had developed. Through this approach, questionnaires from 3,499 children and adolescents between the ages of 8 and 20 were obtained. The sample is by no means representative for the general West German youth population: Already the fact that cooperation partners were almost exclusively individuals close to the peace movement, does create a difficult to quantify pro-peace-movement bias. Also, the bell-shaped age distribution of the sample (with a mean close to 14) speaks against the representativeness of the sample, as West German birth cohorts born between 1965 and 1977, the birth years of our study participants, are about equally sized, so that in a representative sample there should be similar numbers of participants per birth year. Furthermore, the original cross-sectional sample had more *Gymnasium* students, that is, students from the highest German school track, than one would expect in a normal sample. No deviations from frequencies typical for a representative sample were found for region of residence within the old West Germany or for gender. Between Waves 1 and 2, the Chernobyl nuclear catastrophe had happened.

Of all participants who had been surveyed in 1985, 1,492 left their addresses. Of the 1,492 potential panel participants, 837 (56%) individuals indeed participated in the first follow-up. It would be inappropriate to calculate an attrition rate of 44% from these figures, because participants of the first wave had not been solicited beforehand to participate in a study with regular follow-ups. They had only left their addresses to receive information about the results of the first wave of the study, and were only in 1988 asked whether they would be willing to participate in the present and future follow-ups. However, even an attrition rate of 44% is not extraordinarily high for a panel study with a 3½-year intermission between data gathering waves, working with an unattended sample in Germany at that time (Schneider & Edelstein, 1990). In the follow-up, the percentage of female participants increased to 56%, that is, girls were more prone to participate in the panel than boys. The panel sample proved to be an even more highly educated sample than the original cross-sectional sample. Some 56% came from the highest school track or had already entered a university or college. On average, participants now were 17½ years old. Between Waves 2 and 3, the Berlin Wall had come down, and the first war with Iraq had taken place.

In summer 1992, after another 3½ years, panel participants were approached again. This time 541 individuals between the ages of 14 and 26 (average 21) participated (65% of the participants of the second wave of data gathering). Female participation rates increased slightly to 58%. The trend towards institutions of higher tertiary education continued.

Three hundred and sixty-seven participants filled in questionnaires in the fourth wave of data gathering in the winter of 1995/1996 (68% of the participants of the third wave). They were now between 18 and 30 years old (average = 24.7). Male participation rates stabilized at 43%. During the surveying, military action in abundance took place on the Balkans.

Then being between 21 and 34 years old (average = 28.2), 241 individuals (65% of the participants of the fourth wave) participated in the fifth wave of data gathering in 1999. The gender distribution remained stable. Between the fourth and the fifth wave of data gathering, the war around Kosovo took place.

Eighty-three percent of the participants of the fifth wave participated again in the sixth wave, 201 individuals. The female participation rate went up to 61%. Also, the upward educational bias, which had always existed, increased continuously. Only slightly more than 15% of the participants of the sixth wave did not obtain the *Abitur* school-leaving certificate. It also has to be remembered that participants of this study are West Germans only, as in 1985 it was not possible to even snowball into East Germany.[1]

The development of the sample is summarized below in Table 1.

Instruments

To explore psychosocial and health-related consequences of the nuclear threat, an instrument was originally constructed that exclusively encompassed items used before in international studies. In the course of the 20 years for which the study has now been conducted, new foci emerged and new scales and a few open questions were introduced; other items were omitted. In the following section, only those items are reported that are of interest for this analysis.

---

[1]There is one East German participant who somehow managed to get her questionnaire mailed to West Germany in the mid 1980s, when postal controls by the East German secret service were very common.

TABLE 1
Sample Development of the Longitudinal Study "Life Under Nuclear
Threat"

Wave	Time of Data Gathering	N	Retention Rate (%)	Age Range (Average)	Female Participation (%)
1	Summer 1985	1492[a]		8–20 (14.5/13.9)[b]	54
2	Winter 1988/99	837	56	11–23 (17.7/17.5)	56
3	Summer 1992	541	65	14–26 (21.3/21.1)	58
4	Winter 1995/96	367	68	18–30 (24.7/24.7)	57
5	Summer 1999	241	65	21–34 (28.5/28.2)	58
6	Winter 2002/03	201	83	24–35 (31.7/31.7)	61

[a]Of 3,499 children and adolescents surveyed in the cross-sectional study of 1985, 1,492 had left their addresses. [b]The left mean age indicates the mean age of all participants in the pertinent wave of data gathering, whereas the second mean age is the mean age of the core panel sample of the 201 participants who took part in all six waves of data gathering.

After a few sociodemographic questions (*age, gender, school track/type of school-leaving certificate,* and *money available per month*) participants of the study were asked to fill in a checklist of worries of a personal and a political nature, micro- and macrosocial worries. This instrument, introduced by Goldenring and Doctor (1983; 1986), was first used in its original form and later adapted. The original scale encompassed 20 items, the revised version (Boehnke, Schwartz, Stromberg, & Sagiv, 1998) had 35 items. Five items pertaining to such worries as "environmental destruction worsening" or "people in the world dying of hunger" constituted the macrosocial worry scale. Respondents were asked to rate their degree of worry on a 4-point (Wave 1 to Wave 3), later 5-point rating scale (Wave 4 to Wave 6) ranging from 0 (*not worried*) to $3/4^2$ (*greatly worried*). Cronbach's α consistency coefficient for the macrosocial worry scale varied between .63 in 1985 and .77 in 2002/03.

In Waves 2 to 6, participants were asked for their value orientations in line with Inglehart's (1977) conceptualization of materialist versus postmaterialist values, which he later reformulated as measuring self-actualization, as opposed to survival values. To do this in a form that could be used for respondents as young as 11 years (the youngest participants of Wave 2), items from a scale introduced by the first author were used (Boehnke, 1988). For this analysis, only one item could be included to measure self-actualization values, namely "Every individual is obliged to do something for the preservation of the environment." The item had to be answered on a 4-point rating scale, ranging from 0 (*not at all true*) to 3 (*entirely true*).

---

[2]For descriptive purposes, scores from Waves 1 to 3 were multiplied by 1.25 to make them compatible to scores from Waves 4 to 6.

Knowledge about the nuclear threat was measured by posing four multiple choice questions, for example, "In case a city with more than 100,000 inhabitants would be attacked in a nuclear war, how many inhabitants do you think would be left dead or injured? less than 1,000; between 10,000 and 50,000; more than 50,000; don't know." Participants could get up to 4 points on this scale. For this indicator, Guttman's λ was .62 in 1985 (α = .59) and .59 in 1988/1989 (α = .47).

Another set of items used in Waves 1 to 3 focused on intentional aspects of nuclear threat. This instrument was based on work by Goldenring and Doctor (1986), Wahlström (1984), Holmberg and Bergström (1984) and Solantaus, Rimpelä and Taipale (1984). Its thrust was to measure conative involvement with the nuclear threat. All items were "I" statements, and again had to be answered on a 4-point rating scale ranging from 0 (*not at all true*) to 3 (*entirely true*). In this analysis, three items like "I often talk with my friends about the danger of a nuclear war" were used. The consistencies of this scale varied between α = .56 in 1985 and α = .63 in 1988/1989.

Political interest and participation was inquired at the end of the questionnaire in all waves of data gathering. In Waves 1 and 2, participants were, among others, asked whether they had participated in activities of the peace movement in a dichotomous "yes–no" question. Participants were also asked whether their parents had participated in activities of the peace movement. Beginning with Wave 3, participants were asked to what degree they are politically interested and active: "Which of the following sentences describes your political engagement best? (a) I am interested in politics and consider myself an activist (3), (b) I am interested in politics but not active myself (2), (c) I am not very interest in politics, it's one thing among many (1), and (d) I have no interest in politics whatsoever (0)." This item serves as a measure of political engagement.

RESULTS

The presentation of results has two parts. Part 1 documents means and stability coefficients of all variables pertinent to this report. Part 2 reports the findings of two multiple regression analyses with political engagement in 2002 as the dependent variable. The first regression analysis reports the predictive power of sociodemographic variables, as well as concurrent self-actualization values and macrosocial worries as predictors. The second analysis continues by presenting multiple regression analyses with the same dependent variable, political engagement in 2002, but now using predictors from Wave 1 or the earliest possible wave for variables that were only introduced after Wave 1.

Stability and Change in the Ratings

Before reporting concurrent and long-term prediction of political participation, it seems appropriate to briefly look at stability and change in the ratings of items used for this report. Table 2 reports means and stability coefficients for all variables used in the regression analyses of this article.

The table shows, first of all, that the general level of political engagement did not drop among the highly cognitively mobilized individuals that constitute our sample. What did decrease is the number of participants being active; that is, actually engaging in political behavior. In 1985, well over one-third of the sample reported having participated in activities of the peace movement, however, in 2002 just 7% of the sample describe themselves as being interested in politics and active. What also becomes evident is that political engagement is to some degree an on-and-off behavior; it is not stable once and for all. Even if one attributes the low stability between Waves 2 and 3 predominantly to the change in the measurement instrument, a certain fluctuation across the years is still obvious. There are, in fact, only two participants (1%) who report active political participation in each and every wave.

Self-actualization values also are not overly stable in adolescence and young adulthood years. The preference of postmaterialistic values seemingly drops at the end of adolescence, and then remains fairly stable in mean endorsements, although positional stability is not overly high; some participants who originally had high postmaterialism values later had low scores and vice versa. This means that individuals can refute their earlier postmaterialistic values, as well as acquire them only in young adulthood.

Of the long-term measures, macrosocial worries, having dropped in means, are the relatively most stable variable. Measurements from two waves—separated by 3½ years—have up to 52% common variance. This means that emotional involvement with the macrosocial sphere seems to be learned fairly early and remains fairly stable during adolescence and young adulthood.

Predicting Political Engagement

Having documented change, we now turn to the prediction of political engagement. As was briefly explicated in the introduction, political psychology sees political engagement predominantly as a consequence of cognitive mobilization plus an impact of the sociodemographic and structural context in which an individual lives. What measures cognitive mobilization best is, however, disputed. In Wave 6, two measures of cognitive mobilization, namely self-actualization values and macrosocial worries, were obtained from participants. Together with sociodemographic information on age, gender, educational level, and financial situation of the respondent, they were entered into a hierarchic multiple regression analysis; sociodemographic variables were entered first, followed by values and worries in two different steps.

TABLE 2
Means and Stability Coefficients for all Variables Used in Regression Analysis[a]

	Mean 1985	r 85→88	Mean 1988/9	r 88→92	Mean 1992	r 92→95	Mean 1995/6	r 95→99	Mean 1999	r 99→02	Mean 2002/3
Educational Attainment[b] $F = 44.6, p < .001$[c] $F_1 = 110.7, p < .001$	54.2	.50	55.2	.42	60.7	.52	83.6	.86	83.6	.87	84.1
Financial Resources $F = 128.1, p < .001$ $F_1 = 173.9, p < .001$	—	—	—	—	—	—	708.52	.51	1072.40	.38	1726.32
Parental Political Engagement[d] $F = 3.7, p = .055$	36.8	.66	42.3	—	—	—	—	—	—	—	—
Self-Actualization Values $F=16.5, p < .001$ $F_1 = 44.5, p < .001$	—	—	2.93	.28	2.93	.15	2.76	.40	2.72	.34	2.72
Macrosocial Worries $F = 9.6, p < .01$ $F_1 = 16.0, p < .001$	2.21[e]	.39	2.30[e]	.41	2.13[c]	.54	2.24	.72	2.08	.64	2.00

Knowledge about Nuclear Threat[f] $F = 51.0, p < .001$	2.69	.46	3.15	—	—	—	—	—	—	—
Cognitive Involvement $F = 28.0, p < .001$ $F_l = 49.5, p < .001$	1.04	.39	.88	.40	.68	—	—	—	—	—
Political Engagement $F = .99, p = .321$ $F = 36.7, p < .001$[i] $F_l = 80.7, p < .001$	1.69[g] (34.8)[h]	.42	1.72 (35.8)	.17	1.82 (10.4)	.53	1.75 (9.5)	.69	1.74 (8.0)	.44	1.81 (7.0)

[a]All analyses are based on a data set where missing values have been substituted by using EM imputation. [b]In percentage of participants who attend or have completed the highest school track. [c]First F-coefficient reports overall F for the repeated measures factor, second F-coefficient reports the F for the linear trend component. [d]Percentage of parents who have participated in activities of the peace movement. [e]To adjust for different lengths of rating scales (4-point in Waves 1 to 3, 5-point in Waves 4–6) scores from Waves 4–6 were multiplied by 1.25. [f]Indicating how many of four questions could be answered correctly. [g]Dichotomous rating from Waves 1 and 2 were first coded into 0 for no activity in the peace movement and 3 for yes, having participated in activities of the peace movement, 0 scores were then substituted by randomly assigning scores from a uniform distribution with 0 as the minimum and 2 as the maximum, and rounding these scores to whole integers ranging from 0 to 2. This procedure was undertaken, to make the measure used in Waves 1 and 2 compatible to the 0 to 3 ratings from Waves 3 through 6. [h]Percentage of participants politically active. [i]This F-coefficient pertains to the repeated measures analysis for active versus nonactive participation.

TABLE 3
Results of a Multiple Regression Analysis Predicting Political Engagement
Through Concurrent Predictors

Predictor	Step 1	Step 2	Step 3
Age	.07 (.10*)[a]	.07	.03
Gender	.03 (.06)	.05	.08
Level of educational attainment in 2002	.03 (.04)	.02	.04
Financial resources available per month in 2002	.12 (.15**)	.10	.12
Self-actualization values 2002		.13* (.14**)	.08
Macrosocial worries 2002			.16** (.16**)
	$R^2 = 2.8\%$	$R^2 = 4.4\%$*	$R^2 = 6.3\%$**

[a]Figures in parentheses report zero-order correlations.
$*p < .10. **p < .05.$

Table 3 gives an overview of the standardized regression coefficients and zero-order correlations, R^2 values, and significances of R^2 changes between the steps.

What the table shows is that current sociodemographic circumstances have little impact on the degree of political engagement of participants of this study. Self-actualization values have some predictive capacity, as do macrosocial worries. The latter are clearly the stronger predictor than self-actualization values when both are entered into the regression equation. The multiple correlation of the predictors and the dependent variable political engagement is significant at the 5% level but, taken together, only 6.3% of the variance of political engagement are explained by sociodemographic context and concurrent cognitive mobilization.

Let us now turn to long-term prediction of political engagement. In our second regression analysis, the dependent variable remained the same but this time predictors were taken from Wave 1 (or the earliest wave after that, for measures that were only included in later waves) to test the long-term predictive capacity of the variables included in this study. Table 4 reports the results of a six-step hierarchical regression analysis.

Table 4 documents that approximately 12% of the variance in political engagement in 2003 can be explained on the grounds of predictors, some of which were measured as many as 18 years before. Again it becomes clear that, for this sample, sociodemographic variables are of no import. However, it may be seen as somewhat surprising that early political participation (one's own having participated in activities of the peace movement) and a parental role model (parent's having participated in activities of the peace movement in 1985) does not have any impact on

TABLE 4
Results of a Multiple Regression Analysis Predicting Political Engagement
Through Time-Lagged Predictors

Predictor	Step 1	Step 2	Step 3	Step 4	Step 5	Step 6
Age	.09ᵃ (.10*)	.09	.10	.10	.07	.01
Gender	.05 (.06)	.05	.05	.07	.04	.05
Level of educational attainment 1985	.04 (.07)	.04	.03	.05	.04	.06
Financial resources available per month 1995/6	−.01 (.04)	.00	−.01	.01	.01	.04
Own political engagement 1985		.04 (.04)	.03	−.04	−.05	−.09
Parental political engagement 1985		.02ᵃ (.02)	.02	.03	.03	.03
Self-actualization values 1988			−.12* (.12**)	−.10	−.10	−.10
Macrosocial worries 1985				.25***ᵃ (.23***)	.25***	.19**
Knowledge about nuclear threat 1985					.14* (.17***)	.13*
Conative involvement with nuclear threat 1985						.16*ᵃ (.21***)
	R^2 = 1.4%	R^2 = ᵃ1.7%	R^2 = 3.0%	R^2 = 8.6%**	R^2 = 10.2%**	R^2 = 11.9%**

ᵃ Figures in parentheses report zero-order correlations.
*$p < .10$. **$p < .05$. ***$p < .01$.

political engagement in 2002. It is also surprising that self-actualization values held at the age of 17 (on average) do not predict current political engagement. The relationship even is negative. This means that the degree to which an adolescent holds postmaterialistic value orientations does not predict that adolescent's later political engagement and, if it does, it does so negatively. Emotional (worries), cognitive (knowledge), and conative (intentional) involvement with political issues at around 14, however, are fairly strong predictors of political engagement in a participant's early 30s.[3]

---

[3]It should be mentioned here that logistic regression analyses with active political behavior as the dependent variable are similar in their results. Here, however, only macrosocial worries come out as a significant predictor.

DISCUSSION

First of all, readers may be interested in how the title question can be answered. Evidence from our study is clear in this respect. "No." Having engaged in peace movement activities very early in life, or having had a parental role model who has engaged in activities of the peace movement, will not "do the trick." Judging from the data presented here, it does not pay to have young people attend short-term political events. In a representative sample, it might have shown that young people who attended political events in adolescence are also the politically more active adults, but within a group of sympathizers with the goals of the peace movement (we can be fairly sure that this is the case for the vast majority of our sample) early "peace behavior" is not what counts. Parents who "drag" their children to peace movement events must accept that this neither harms nor fosters future engagement in politics.

Something else is much more important, and that is indeed what Inglehart (1977) labeled cognitive involvement. However, values, as he defines them, do not seem to be a very good measure of cognitive mobilization among adolescents. Of course, one should interject that the measurement of self-actualization values through one item was quite imperfect but the fact that none of the 12 items in the value scale used from 1988 onwards had a significant long-term predictive power supports the interpretation that values measured in adolescence are not a good predictor of later political engagement.

What turns out to be a much better predictor of long-term political engagement is the emotional, cognitive, and conative involvement with the political sphere. Youngsters who worry a lot about what goes on in the world early in their lives, who know a lot about hot political topics, and who engage a lot in prepolitical behavior, such as discussing matters of political interest with their peers and their parents, are highly prone to become politically active adults, even if they do not engage in concrete political behavior in adolescence.

Thus, to foster the raising of politically active citizens, parents need not take their children to political events. What is necessary is that they assist their children in being or becoming concerned, that they talk politics with them, and that they increase the political knowledge of their offspring. Peter Hofstätter's 1985 accusation that IPPNW physicians were frightening children may indeed have had some substance, because IPPNW, and with it the initiators of this study, pointed to some really frightening things going on in the political sphere. By doing this, however, IPPNW did by no means inject "No future" into the younger generation, but did, indeed, exactly the opposite. It laid the ground for active political engagement in adulthood. The most worried adolescents of the mid-1980s tend to be most politically active adults of today.

Of course, this study rightfully draws a number of methodological criticisms. First, measurement of value orientations was far from being perfect. Second, the sample is not a sample representative of the West German, notwithstanding all-German, adolescent population. Third, the large number of dropouts the study experienced over the years is puzzling. Would the relationship between predictors and dependent variable have been substantially different from what was found for the continuing participants of the study? There is little evidence that this would have been the case. Earlier publications relying on data up to Wave 4 (Sohr, Boehnke, & Stromberg, 1998), or up to Wave 5 (Boehnke, Fuß, & Rupf, 2000) reported, in essence, the same findings, in spite of the fact that they included higher numbers of participants, namely those who dropped out after Wave 4 or Wave 5, in addition to the present participants.

From a developmental psychology point of view, it should additionally be highlighted that the explanatory power of predictors from 15 to 18 years before the sixth wave of measurement is higher than the predictive power of concurrent measures. The change in explained variance generated by the inclusion of macrosocial worries into the regression equation, for example, is 1.9% for concurrent worries; it is 5.6% for worries experienced 18 years back.

All in all, one can reiterate that it is not so important to show early behavioral engagement, but what has the decisive impact on later political engagement is early cognitive involvement in politics.

ACKNOWLEDGMENTS

This study was financed by the International Physicians for the Prevention of Nuclear War (IPPNW), Boston, Nobel Peace Prize awardee in 1985, the German Section of this organization ("Ärzte in sozialer Verantwortung"), Freudenberg Foundation, the Gruner & Jahr and the Rudolf Augstein publishing companies, Berlin University of Technology, the Free University of Berlin, Chemnitz University of Technology, and the International University Bremen.

Over the years the following colleagues have worked on the study: Michael J. Macpherson, Margarete Meador, Horst Petri, Egbert von Fromberg, Sven Sohr, Sabine Zöge, Peggy Turek, Claudia Stromberg, Daniel Fuß, Janina Marguć, and Yavor Braytchev.

BIOGRAPHICAL NOTES

Klaus Boehnke, born 1951, studied English, Russian, and Psychology; PhD in psychology, Berlin University of Technology, 1985; assistant/associate professor, Department of Education, Free University of Berlin; full Professor of Socialization Research, Department of Sociology, Chemnitz University of Technology, 1993–2002; since 2002 Professor of Social Science Methodology, International University Bremen. His research interests lie in the field of youth research and its methodology.

Mandy Boehnke, born 1976, studied Sociology, Psychology, and Economics, MA in sociology; Chemnitz University of Technology (CUT), 2003; held positions of teaching and research assistant at CUT and at International University Bremen; currently research associate in a family sociology project on "Timing of Parenthood" at the University of Bremen. Her research interest lies in the field of interdisciplinary family research.

REFERENCES

Ardila, R. (1986). The psychological impact of the nuclear threat on the Third World: The case of Colombia. *International Journal of Mental Health, 15,* 162–171.

Beardslee, W. R., & Mack, J. E. (1983). Adolescents and the threat of nuclear war. The evolution of the perspective. *Yale Journal of Biological Medicine, 56,* 79–91.

Boehnke, K. (1988). *Prosoziale Motivation, Selbstkonzept und politische Orientierung—Entwicklungsbedingungen und Veränderungen im Jugendalter* [Prosocial motivation, self-concept and political orientation—developmental context and change in adolescence]. Frankfurt, Germany: Lang.

Boehnke, K., Fromberg, E.v., & Macpherson, M.J. (1992). Macro-social stress in adolescence: Results of follow-up survey on war anxiety and anxiety of environmental destruction. *Psychiatry Digest, 6,* 18–19.

Boehnke, K., Fuß, D., & Rupf, M. (2000). Die Kinder der Friedensbewegung: Wege in die Politikverdrossenheit? [The children of the peace movement: Paths into political alienation?] In H.-P. Kuhn, H. Uhlendorff, & L. Krappmann (Eds.), *Sozialisation zur Mitbürgerlichkeit* (pp. 113–131). Opladen, Germany: Leske + Budrich.

Boehnke, K., Fuß, D., & Rupf, M. (2001). Values and well-being: The mediating role of worries. In P. Schmuck, & K. Sheldon (Eds.), *Life goals and well-being* (pp. 95–101). Seattle, WA: Hogrefe & Huber.

Boehnke, K., Macpherson, M., Meador, M., & Petri, H. (1989). How German adolescents experience the nuclear threat. *Political Psychology, 10,* 419–443.

Boehnke, K., Schwartz, S.H., Stromberg, C., & Sagiv, L. (1998). The Structure and dynamics of worry: Theory, measurement and cross-national replications. *Journal of Personality, 66,* 745–782.

Claussen, B., & Geissler, R. (1996). *Die Politisierung des Menschen. Instanzen politischer Sozialisation* [The politicization of man: Entities of political socilization]. Opladen, Germany: Westdeutscher Verlag.

Gabriel, O. W. (1986). *Politische Kultur, Postmaterialismus und Materialismus in der Bundesrepublik Deutschland* [Political culture, postmaterialism and materialism in the Federal Republic of Germany]. Opladen, Germany: Westdeutscher Verlag.

Gabriel, O. W. (1997). *Politische Orientierungen und Verhaltensweisen im vereinigten Deutschland* [Political orientations and modes of political behavior in the united Germany]. Opladen, Germany: Leske + Budrich.

Gaiser, W., de Rijke, J., & Wächter, F. (2003). Germany. In M. Taru (Ed.), *Political participation of young people in Europe—development of indicators for comparative research in the European Union* (pp. 34–37). Vienna: EUYOUPART. Retrieved May 8, 2004 from http:www.sora.at/objects/stateoftheart.pdf.

Gille, M., Krüger, W., de Rijke, J., & Willems, H. (1998). Politische Orientierung, Werthaltungen und die Partizipation Jugendlicher: Veränderungen und Trends in den 90er Jahren [Political orientation, value orientations, and the participation of adolescents: Changes and trends in the 1990s]. In C. Palentien & K. Hurrelmann (Eds.), *Jugend und Politik. Ein Handbuch für Forschung, Lehre und Praxis* (pp. 148–177). Neuwied, Germany: Luchterhand.

Goldenring, J. M., & Doctor, R. (1983). *Adolescent concerns about nuclear war.* Los Angeles: unpublished manuscript.

Goldenring, J. M., & Doctor, R. (1986). Teenage worry about nuclear war: North-American and European questionnaire studies. *International Journal of Mental Health, 15,* 72–92.

Hoffmann-Lange, U. (1998). Jugend zwischen politischer Teilnahmebereitschaft und Politikverdrossenheit [Youth between political participation motivation and alienation]. In C. Palentien & K. Hurrelmann (Eds.), *Jugend und Politik. Ein Handbuch für Forschung, Lehre und Praxis* (pp. 178–205). Neuwied, Germany: Luchterhand.

Hofstätter, P. R. (1985, November 15). Kindern Angst machen [Frightening children]. *Die Welt,* p. 2.

Holmberg, P. O., & Bergström, A. (1984, June). *How Swedish teenagers aged 13–15 think and feel concerning the nuclear threat.* Paper presented at the 4th Congress of the International Physicians for the Prevention of Nuclear War, Espoo, Finland.

Inglehart, R. (1977). *The silent revolution.* Princeton, NJ: Princeton University Press.

Klingemann, H.-D., & Kaase, M. (1981). *Politische Psychologie* [Political Psychology]. Opladen, Germany: Westdeutscher Verlag.

Krampen, G. (1991). Political participation in an action-theory model of personality: Theory and empirical evidence. *Political Psychology, 12,* 1–25.

Krampen, G. (2000). Transition of adolescent political action orientations to voting behavior in early adulthood in view of a social-cognitive action theory model of personality. *Political Psychology, 21,* 277–297.

Lazarus, R. S., & Folkman, S. (1984). *Stress, appraisal and coping.* New York: Springer.

Mair, P., & van Biezen, I. (2001). Party membership in twenty European democracies 1980–2000. *Party Politics, 7,* 5–22.

Meyer-Probst, B., Teichmann, H., & Kleinpeter, U. (1989). Psychische Widerspiegelungen der atomaren Bedrohung bei Jugendlichen [Psychological repercussions of the nuclear threat among adolescents]. *Ärztliche Jugendkunde, 80,* 228–236.

Newcomb, M. D. (1986). Nuclear attitudes and reactions: Associations with depression, drug use, and quality of life. *Journal of Personality and Social Psychology, 50,* 906–920.

Newcomb, M. D. (1988). Nuclear anxiety and psychosocial functioning among young adults. *Basic & Applied Social Psychology, 9,* 107–134.

Oswald, H. (1998). Socialisation und Entwicklung in den neuen Bundesländern [Socialization and development in the new states of Germany]. Special issue of *Zeitschrift für Soziologie der Erziehung und Sozialisation.* Weinheim, Germany: Juventa.

Oswald, H. (1999). Political socialization in the new states of Germany. In M. Yates & J. Youniss (Eds.), *Roots of civic identity. International perspectives on community service and activism in youth* (pp. 97–113). Cambridge: University Press.

Oswald, H., & Schmid, C. (1998). Poltical participation of young people in East Germany. *German Politics, 7,* 147–164.

Palentien, C., & Hurrelmann, K. (Eds.) (1998). *Jugend und Politik. Ein Handbuch für Forschung, Lehre und Praxis.* Neuwied, Germany: Luchterhand.

Reinders, H. (2003). Politische sozialisation in der Adoleszenz: Eine Reinterpretation quantitativer Längsschnittuntersuchungen in Deutschland [Political socialization in adolescence: A reinterpretation of quatitative panel studies in Germany]. *Zeitschrift für Entwicklungspsychologie und pädagogische psychologie, 35,* 98–110.

Schmitt, H. (2005). The European Parliament elections of June 2004: Still second-order? Manheim: MZWS. Retrieved July 22, 2005, from http://www.mzes.uni-manheim.de/publications/papers/HS_EP_ParlElec_2004.pdf

Schneider, W., & Edelstein, W. (1990). *European inventory of longitudinal studies in the behavioral and medical sciences.* Munich, Germany: Max Planck Institiute for Psychological Research.

Sohr, S., Boehnke, K., & Stromberg, C. (1998) "Politische Persönlichkeiten"—Eine aussterbende spezies? ["Political personalities"—A dying species?] In C. Palentien & K. Hurrelmann (Hg.), *Jugend und Politik. Ein Handbuch für Forschung, Lehre und Praxis* (pp. 206–235). Neuwied, Germany: Luchterhand.

Solantaus, T., Rimpelä, M., & Taipale, V. (1984). The nuclear war in the minds of 12-to-18-year-olds in Finland. *Lancet, 8380,* 784–785.

Sommers, F. G., Goldberg, S., Levinson, D., Ross, C., & LaCombe, S. (1985): Children's mental health and the threat of nuclear war: A Canadian pilot study. In T. Solantaus, E. Chivian, M. Vartanyan, & S. Chivian (Eds.), *Impact of the threat of nuclear war on children and adolescents* (pp. 61–93). Boston: International Physicians for the Prevention of Nuclear War.

Taru, M. (2003). *Political participation of young people in Europe—development of indicators for comparative research in the European Union.* Vienna: EUYOUPART. Retrieved May 8, 2005 from http:www.sora.at/objects/stateoftheart.pdf.

Wahlström, R. (1984). Fear of war, conceptions of war, and peace activities: Their relation to self-esteem in young people. In T. Solantaus, E. Chivian, M. Vartanyan, & S. Chivian (Eds.), *Impact of the threat of nuclear war on children and adolescents* (pp. 104–111). Boston: International Physicians for the Prevention of Nuclear War.

Wasilewski, B. (1989). Die psychologischen und gesundheitlichen Folgen der Angst vor einem Atomkrieg bei Watrschauer Jugendlichen [The psychological and health-related consequences of anxiety about a nuclear war among Warsaw adolescents]. In K. Boehnke, M. J. Macpherson, & F. Schmidt (Eds.), *Leben unter atomarer Bedrohung—Ergebnisse internationaler psychologischer Forschung* (pp. 149–162). Heidelberg, Germany: Asanger.

PEACE AND CONFLICT: JOURNAL OF PEACE PSYCHOLOGY, *11*(3), 355–365

Refugees in Church Asylum: Intervention Between Political Conflict and Individual Suffering

Ingrid I. Koop
REFUGIO Bremen, Germany

Work with refugees in church asylum is an example of applied Peace Psychology that considers the interaction between wider collective conflicts and their manifestations in individual lives. This article presents the qualitative study of a Kurdish refugee couple who stayed 8 months in church asylum. The case opens by describing the couple's political sufferings in Turkey and Germany. It continues with an account of their asylum saga and the numerous everyday challenges they confront. Political strategies in support of the asylum issue entail addressing legal accusations, creating positive political identities in the public mind, and expanding the support group. Psychological interventions must be politically sensitive to the asylum-seekers' history and current context. Effective psychological interventions include relaxation, framing a political meaning for suffering, creating a home–country cultural atmosphere, and processing trauma.

When a refugee fearing deportation seeks shelter in a church, the Church may decide to temporarily host the refugee in church rooms, an act traditionally known as church asylum. Through this act, the refugee and his or her group of supporters gain time to press the authorities to reconsider the refugee's situation, taking into account all legal, social, and humanitarian aspects. Church asylum is always *ultima ratio* (a last resort), because the process demands much courage and energy from all of the participants involved, requiring moves outside the boundaries of legally accepted behavior. It is usually justified only if deportation would jeopardize the refugee's life or freedom.

Just and Straeter (2003, pp. 14–17) described the right of asylum as one of the oldest human rights. It is believed to have existed for over 3,500 years, and has religious roots. Protection by asylum—at holy statues, temples, graves, and other sacred places—has been found in many ancient cultures. The Greek words *asylos*

Requests for reprints should be sent to Ingrid Koop, Heidelberger Str. 13, 28203 Bremen, Germany. E-mail: koopingrid@yahoo.de

topos suggest a sacred place from which it is forbidden to remove persons or things. Breaking this sacred sphere of protection was not only against the law but was considered a great cultural taboo. The Christian churches continued with the idea of asylum formerly practiced by Roman temples. It is known that, as early as the 4th century A.D., persecuted people found temporary shelter in churches. In European medieval times, Christian asylum was considered legitimate protection in a holy site, with the altar as a source of shelter for the innocently persecuted. However, with the founding of the modern constitutional state in the 18th and 19th centuries, church asylum dissolved as an explicit right (Just & Straeter, 2003, p.17).

Today, a number of Christian communities in Germany have taken up the ancient tradition of sheltering asylum-seekers. The process of protecting refugees in churches, however, falls under the jurisdiction of secular constitutions. Christian asylum providers are expected by law to act as citizens in a constitutional society and to deal with social conflicts in legally acceptable ways. Situations where the executive considers the asylum illegal provide a challenge to both the asylum providers on the one hand and the state forces on the other. The police have the constitutional duty to remove refugees from churches, yet such moves are normally avoided because of disproportionately strong counteractions and protests from culturally influential Christian communities. More than 550 examples are known to have taken place in Germany since the first Berlin church asylum in 1983. Many cases were successful, resulting in a revision of decisions on the refugees' status and, in more than 70% of the cases, preventing deportation of the asylum-seekers (on success or failure of church asylum, also see Straeter, 2003).

CONTEXTUAL AND SUBJECTIVE DIMENSIONS OF ASYLUM-SEEKING

A psychological understanding of church asylum in Germany makes a two-pronged consideration of both political context and individual subjectivities necessary. More specifically, this involves examining the consequences for the asylum seeker of the interface between state political procedures and decisions and individual political perceptions and practices. Further, psychological interventions with asylum-seekers aim to counter harmful political conflicts in the refugee's home country, as well as in the country of exile, Germany. The problematic context in the home country usually has to do with a repressive regime, and difficulties in Germany involve dealing with government legal and police forces that aim to send asylum seekers back to their home country.

During asylum seeking, context and subjectivity constantly influence each other in a bi-directional relationship. Contextual conditions include considerations related to the constitution and other legal codes, media and public relations related to social persuasion, and social networking around the asylum issue. These external circumstances interact constantly with human subjectivities, which include culturally supported ethical standards and the psychological dynamics of actors involved in the asylum issue. This article now proceeds to discuss each aspect of asylum seeking, separately.

Political Context of Asylum Seeking in Germany

The right to asylum is laid down in Article 16 of the German constitution. Originally, this right was a genuine constitutional right not restricted by a special law. However, for some 15 years now the right to asylum has been curbed by an Asylum Law that lays down the guideline for legal authorities. However, because the execution of this law varies widely, depending on the political interest of federal and state governments, the outcome of an asylum seeker's case can be shaped by lobbying pressures on politicians by refugees and human rights organizations, compatriots, and other groups sympathetic to asylum seekers.

The concrete legal level of an asylum case involves the refugee authorities, immigration authorities, and a chamber of the administrative court as instruments of governance, as well as lawyers of the refugees' supporters. As soon as an asylum issue arises, it is highly advisable to consult a lawyer experienced in asylum law and foreigners' rights, and to involve him or her in the church asylum process. Investigations have to be made by gathering thorough information on the person, the home country, the reasons for the seeking of refuge, and the legal status of the case. Sometimes, it can be useful to establish church asylum until this information is complete. It is especially important to concretize reasonable and realistic perspectives to avoid false hopes and promises to the refugee, as well as frustration and loss of motivation among supporters.

Another significant factor in the refugee's social situation is the intensity of public relations utilized to sway the community toward the side of the asylum seeker. Print media, radio, and television, as well as public events and activities, can generate mass sympathy for the refugee, favoring church protection rather than deportation. Other persuasive messages relayed through public relations drives include calls to limit police intervention, demands that court and other involved authorities investigate the case further, and reopening of legal proceedings, which can serve to delay the pending deportation.

A refugee's social network serves as a vital sustaining force. This support group may consist of family members, friends, compatriots, and supporters of the church community. They not only compensate for the refugee's limited resources, but also bring the asylum issue out into the public arena. Support groups assist in operations, material needs, and moral support. They help organize the refugee's everyday life, back up legal procedures, and do public relations work. A support group can also provide temporary shelter for asylum seekers, and generate financial resources. Finally, support groups' community prayers provide encouragement to persist, in spite of the difficulties involved in the asylum-seeking process.

Psychocultural Aspects of Asylum-seeking

Church asylum likewise activates subjective awareness on both the collective and individual levels. One needs to be aware of the ethical dimension of asylum seeking. The political process touches upon sets of cultural and religious beliefs and traditions, as well as human rights values among refugees and their supporters. Moreover, ethical values favoring the asylum seeker's well being may be used to challenge legal decisions and police action supporting deportation. The refugee's mental dispositions may also come into play during the asylum seeking process. Personal supporters and professional psychologists attend to the refugee's motivations, abilities, psychodynamics, expectations, frustrations and mental health. At the outset, it is important to assess a refugee's motivation, will, and ability to deal with the psychological challenges of the arduous process. A common initial question is whether the refugee can bear the situation and is prepared to live only within church premises, in a prison among friends.

The following case of Mr. and Mrs. K.—Kurdish refugees from Turkey who sought church asylum in Germany—demonstrates the dynamic interaction between political context and psychological intervention during asylum seeking. The political contexts in both the home country, Turkey, and refuge country, Germany, created psychological distress in the couple. Their social context in Germany likewise provided positive support for internal healing and political refuge.

POLITICAL AND PSYCHOLOGICAL DIMENSIONS OF ASYLUM-SEEKING: THE CASE OF MR. AND MRS. K.

Political Conflict in Turkey

The history of the Kurdish people in Turkey is characterized by oppression, persecution, and armed conflict. In 1980, the military coup d'etat in Turkey sparked another round of conflict between the Turkish state and Kurdish groups that continued through the 1980s and into the 1990s. The Turkish-Kurdish conflict goes back at least to the time when the Ottoman Empire dissolved and Kurds were promised a nation-state of their own in the Treaty of Versailles, a promise that was reversed in the treaty of Lausanne in 1923 (Nirumand, 1991). The armed conflict between Turkish security forces and the Kurdish Workers' Party (PKK) lasted from 1984 to August 1999, and took place mainly in the Kurd-populated southeast of Turkey. During the conflict, both parties committed human rights abuses, although the more glaring atrocities were carried out by Turkish police and military forces (Yavuz, 1999).

During the conflict, an estimated 4,500 civilians were killed, approximately 3,000 Kurdish settlements were evacuated or burned down, and up to 3 million people suffered internal displacement. House-to-house-searches, torching of residences, detention, torture, and extrajuridical executions were common practice.

Torture methods included severe beatings, being stripped naked and blindfolded, hosing with pressurized ice-cold water, hanging by the arms or wrists bound behind the victim's back, electroshock torture, beating the soles of the feet, death threats, and sexual assaults including rape. Among the victims were PKK fighters, Kurdish civilians, opposition politicians, villagers, and socially disadvantaged groups; victims included children, women, and elderly people (Amnesty International, 2000). Since 1999, the situation has improved but the Turkish government continues to tolerate persecution, detention, and torture.

Many Kurds fled to safer places, like Western Turkey and other European countries. In the 1990s, Germany was one of the main destinations for Kurdish refugees. By 1999, approximately 600,000 Kurdish people had sought refuge in Germany (Ammann, 1999). The story of Mr. and Mrs. K. represents a narrative of many other Kurd refugees in the 1990s.

Personal Suffering in Turkey and Germany

Political duress.   Mr. K., 34 years old, and his wife Mrs. K., 27 years old, are Kurds from East Turkey who fled to Germany in 1996. Both had been persecuted in their home country for their political activities. Mrs. K. was maltreated during different violent house visits and interrogations by the military. Mr. K. was in detention several times, and had been severely tortured. In Germany, both applied for political asylum. Although the fact of political persecution was officially acknowledged, the asylum application was rejected by German authorities who gave West Turkey as a flight alternative the couple could have chosen (this was the usual court practice at that time).

In the summer of 2000, the order came to leave Germany. When the German police brought the official expulsion order, Mrs. and Mr. K. relived the traumatic persecution and threatening they had suffered in Turkey. "Suddenly there were again two policemen at our door who wanted to take us away." In panic, they left their home. "We quickly packed our plastic bags, like at that time in Turkey." The couple's illegal situation turned critical as they went undercover to a relative in another town. To aggravate matters, Mrs. K. suffered a miscarriage. They sought help for their poor state of health at a treatment center for traumatized refugees, where I met the couple.

Psychological duress.   Both refugees had suffered traumatic events in their homeland, Turkey. Their situation in Germany had turned into one of extreme uncertainty and threat. They experienced sequential traumatization, an open-ended situation that is most difficult to bear (Keilson, 1979).

Mr. K. suffered sleep disorders and nightmares after his several political detentions, torture, and flight from Turkey. In Germany, these symptoms intensified, and he grew more nervous, irritable, and easily frightened. His physiological hyperarousal was expressed in his severely and almost constantly trembling hands, strong headaches, and backaches. When the German expulsion order was served, Mr. K. experienced this as a traumatic repetition of Turkish detention and torture. He showed a characteristic psychic emergency reaction in the impulse to flee and hide. The hiding—in his perception—seemed to be the only possible escape from a life-threatening emergency situation.

Mrs. K. was more stable than her husband, but also suffered sleep disorders, fear, and anxiety reactions, which increased after her miscarriage. In addition, she developed psychosomatic symptoms like headaches and stomach pain. For her, the expulsion order was also a traumatic repetition of her traumas in Turkey, and she reacted to the acute triggers with increased stress. Two additional mental burdens for her were the uncertain situation of her illegal stay in Germany and the miscarriage of her long-wished-for pregnancy. Losing her unborn child was the worst traumatic event for her. She was on the brink of a psychological breakdown.

The Asylum Begins

Several conditions at that point required an *ultima ratio*, making church asylum a reasonable option. First, the couple's stay in Germany had been deemed illegal. Second, deportation to Turkey would have placed them at risk of another detention and additional torture. Third, Mr. and Mrs. K. were physically and mentally exhausted. The desperate Kurdish couple decided to seek church asylum. After some efforts, a church community was found that already had a working group on asylum and was willing to serve as a support group. They helped organize facilities for the couple's practical needs, like a sleeping area, bathroom access, and use of kitchen facilities. Mr. and Mrs. K. were assisted by an experienced lawyer who was sympathetic to the idea of church asylum and saw the possibility of taking further legal measures if granted more time.

The church asylum situation was characterized by waiting, forced passiveness, and a limited radius of movement. The couple was encouraged to remain in church territory as much as possible, to minimize the risk of being seized by the police. A regular daily schedule was agreed upon by both partners. For example, Mrs. K. prepared meals and assisted in the church kindergarten daily. Later, Mr. K. helped in the little church garden and worked as a janitor.

During church asylum, I met Mr. and Mrs. K. for psychological counseling every week or two, and kept phone contact between visits. Although Mr. K. spoke some German, most of the sessions were assisted by a specially trained interpreter from the treatment center (see also Haenel, 2001). In general, the use of an interpreter enabled work on more complex psychological issues and a wider spectrum of emotions.

Building Political Strength During Asylum Conflict

Addressing legal problems.   One of the first steps in the asylum process was to engage a lawyer who would work collaboratively with Mr. and Mrs. K. Two goals were defined for the church asylum period. The short-term goal was to get the couple back to legal status, so they could return to their house and receive regular payments from social services. The medium-term goal was to reopen—and win—Mr. K.'s court case, on the grounds that his torture experiences and traumatized mental health state had not been sufficiently considered.

After the couple moved to church quarters, they gained an official address, and hence claimed they were legal once again. News about the couple's church asylum was published to make public their official address. The regional minister for inner affairs then called the church asylum illegal, and demanded that Mr. and Mrs. K. leave. Fortunately, the government's contentions remained only verbal, and there were no actual attempts to remove the refugees from their asylum. The case then had to be readdressed by the Federal Authority for Refugees and at court, which was a lengthy process that gained the couple precious time.

Creating positive political identities in the public mind. Supporters of the asylum issue projected Mr. and Mrs. K. as symbolic fighters for Kurdish culture and human rights. Mr. and Mrs. K. gave newspaper and radio interviews on the oppressive situation in Kurdistan, and on their church asylum. Their lawyer and support group organized a public event about the political situation in Kurdistan. The intensification of the couple's political identity as Kurdish refugees generated widespread community support, and brought in much-needed resources from a sympathetic public. In addition to its political and material benefits, their strengthened political identity as Kurdish freedom fighters inspired Mr. and Mrs. K. in their difficult struggle, giving political meaning to their personal sacrifice. Political activities were prepared and reflected on during psychological sessions with the couple, motivating especially Mr. K. by integrating the personal and the political identity. This procedure demonstrated the importance of identity work on trauma (see Koop, 2001).

Expanding the support group. While hiding from German authorities, the social relationships of Mr. and Mrs. K. thinned out to one remaining relative and her family. The creation of a Church back-up group widened their support circle. Other compatriots and like-minded individuals, motivated by humanitarian and solidarity concerns, eventually joined the growing circle of supporters.

Politically Sensitive Psychological Interventions

The psychological interventions were planned in relation to the couple's pragmatic everyday needs and the political demands of their asylum seeking. Mr. and Mrs. K. had to be encouraged to take care of their legal matters, personal health, and daily needs, such as acquiring a mobile phone and obtaining Turkish newspapers. The most urgent psychological interventions had to do with mitigating somatic symptoms, stabilizing and strengthening inner resources, and reflecting on personal consequences of their condition. Confrontation with the original trauma was not indicated as a priority because of their unstable personal and political situation. During church asylum, psychological interventions included the following elements: relaxation techniques, framing a political meaning for suffering, creating a home-country cultural atmosphere, and processing trauma.

Relaxation techniques.   To regulate the physiological hyperarousal characteristic of trauma, some simple body interventions were introduced (for more on the importance of combining body and psychological treatment, see Koop, 2003). The couple started with walks around church territory, and was encouraged to spend some time daily enjoying fresh air. They likewise practiced brief breathing exercises for short-term relaxation. Some playful movement exercises were introduced, like enjoying *indiaca* (an Indian ball game). Mr. K. hesitated somewhat, but his wife engaged in these games enthusiastically. Both were able to concentrate on bodily relaxation for a short time, Mrs. K. more so than her husband. A lasting change of their hyperarousal was not possible because of the continuing tense situation.

Framing a political meaning for suffering.   To activate their own healing process, the couple participated in the cognitive and emotional evaluation of their legal, political, and health situation. Beyond acquiring information about the form and function of their own symptoms, Mr. and Mrs. K. likewise learned to frame their personal suffering in relation to their contextual collective conflict, thus linking the psychological with the political. Mrs. K. understood connections quite quickly, felt a certain relief with it, and sometimes explained the connections again to her husband in her own words.

Creating a home-country cultural atmosphere.   The couple liked to listen to Kurdish music. This was relaxing and produced the positive effect of strengthening their cultural identity. Mrs. K. also took part in the folk dance class of the church community, which relaxed her, raised her mood, and expanded her social contacts. She showed the class a Kurdish folk dance. The Moslem couple was invited and participated in the Christmas service, and at the end of their stay, a Thanksgiving service celebrated with the supporters' group. They talked with the priest, the support group, and me about religion, especially what Allah wanted to teach them by their fate and what the idea of the Moslem and the Christian God had in common.

Processing trauma.   In Germany, the couple had been retraumatized, first by the policemen with the expulsion order at their door, and then by Mrs. K.'s miscarriage, with these incidents triggering memories of their hardships in Turkey. It was relatively easy to process the effect of their encounter with the German police by reflecting on the situation within the context of their whole life history.[1] The topic of miscarriage was much more difficult. Mr. K. was somewhat defensive re-

---

[1]At a meeting about one year later, Mrs. K. reported that there had been a policeman at their door again. This time she had been excited but did not panic.

garding the issue, and pushed for a medical examination to establish that they could begin another pregnancy. But Mrs. K. was depressed and cried a great deal when the issue was discussed with her alone. Psychological reframing helped her balance her feelings and enabled her to develop reality-oriented strategies for handling her distress. Eventually, she agreed with her husband's wish for a medical examination, which showed no medical obstacles to another pregnancy.

A Successful Outcome

Mr. and Mrs. K. were in church asylum for more than eight months. During that time, their legal matters were reviewed by the Federal Authority for Refugees and by the court, which proved to be successful. They were then permitted to return to their former asylum town. A year after the beginning of church asylum, another court hearing took place, and the couple was officially granted political asylum. Another year later, Mrs. K. had stabilized. She had reorganized her life as a housewife and supported her husband practically and emotionally. Mr. K. was still in psychotherapy for the trauma suffered in Turkey and was looking for a job. His desire, as he said, was to "stand on my own feet." Finally, one and a half years after the end of church asylum, Mrs. K. gave birth to a healthy daughter.

FINAL REMARKS

The psychological interventions with Mr. and Mrs. K. required a fine balance by the psychologist between involvement and detachment. Strategies needed to be involved enough to advocate for human life, security, and ethical values, yet distant enough to enable the couple to help themselves. Keeping this balance is a great challenge for the practice of psychological interventions with asylum-seekers.

This article described interventions that addressed the individual needs of Mr. and Mrs. K. Mitigating individual suffering, however, entailed cognitive and power-based engagements within a political-societal context. The single victim must be enabled to perceive himself or herself as part of political persecution and power plays. Only in this way will individual suffering be recognized as not only personal, but also societal. Privately internalized wrongs are reframed and redefined, allowing them to be publicly announced and laid to the society in which they originated. "The only remedy against unwanted intimacy is publication" (Reemtsma, 1997, p. 17, translation by the author). Applying psychological interventions to the church asylum process is a long and difficult task, as psychologists work to initiate, elaborate, and reflect on what they see as the true nature of the individual's suffering. Yet, in the case of Mr. and Mrs. K., it permitted the first steps toward reincorporating the scattered parts of their lives and established a better understanding of the psychological pressures brought upon them by society.

Peltzer (2001) claimed that ethnocultural counseling and psychotherapy with victims of organized violence must derive from an eclectic intervention model. His review of his own work in a trauma center in Frankfurt, Germany, between 1991 and 1995, as well as the work of others, led him to the conclusion that successful psychotherapeutic interventions with traumatized, displaced refugees cannot be carried out within the framework of a rigid "school" approach to psychotherapy. From a scientific point of view, this report of a case of church asylum underscores Peltzer's claim. Psychotherapy with displaced victims of organized violence must incorporate the political and legal situation of the victim in the country where he or she seeks asylum, even more so when they live under the particular conditions of church asylum.

ACKNOWLEDGMENT

The author thanks an anonymous reviewer and the senior editor of this special issue, Klaus Boehnke, as well as the journal editor, Richard Wagner, and associate editor, Cristina Montiel, for very helpful advice offered on earlier versions of this article.

BIOGRAPHICAL NOTE

Ingrid Ingeborg Koop, born 1954, is a practicing psychologist and psychotherapist. She heads the psychotherapy services at REFUGIO Bremen, a treatment center for traumatized refugees and torture survivors. Her areas of specialization include trauma therapy training, integrative movement therapy, and dynamic psychotherapy. She has worked in Latin America and former Yugoslavia. Her research interests lie in psychotraumatology and political and peace psychology.

REFERENCES

Ammann, B. (1999). KurdInnen in der Bundesrepublik Deutschland. [Kurds in the Federal Republic of Germany]. In NAVEND—Zentrum für kurdische Studien e.V. [Center for Kurdish Studies] (Ed.), *KurdInnen in der Bundesrepublik Deutschland—Ein Handbuch [Kurds in the Federal Republic of Germany—A handbook]* (pp. 17—42). Bonn, Germany: NAVEND-Schriftenreihe.

Amnesty International. (2000). *Annual Report*. London: Amnesty International Publications.

Haenel, F. (2001). Ausgewählte Aspekte und Probleme in der Psychotherapie mit Folteropfern unter Beteiligung von Dolmetschern [Selected aspects and problems of psychotherapy with torture victims in presence of interpreters]. In M. Verwey (Ed.), *Trauma und Ressourcen [Trauma and empowerment]*. (Curare Special Volume 16; pp. 307–315). Berlin: Verlag für Wissenschaft und Bildung.

Just, W. D., & Straeter, B. (Eds.). (2003). *Kirchenasyl. Ein Handbuch*. [Church asylum. A handbook]. Karlsruhe, Germany: Von Loeper.

Keilson, H. (1979). *Sequentielle Traumatisierung bei Kindern*. [Sequential traumatization of children]. Stuttgart, Germany: Enke.

Koop, I. (2001). Narben auf der Seele. Integrative Therapie und leibtherapeutische Interventionen in der Arbeit mit Folterüberlebenden. [Scars on the soul. Integrative therapy and body interventions working with torture survivors]. *Integrative Therapie, 4*, 425—458.

Koop, I. (2003, May). *Trauma therapy and the body paradigm*. Paper presented to the VIII European Conference on Traumatic Stress, Berlin.

Nirumand, B. (1991). Die kurdische Tragödie [The Kurdish tragedy]. Reinbek, Germany: Rowohlt.

Peltzer, K. (2001). An integrative model for ethnocultural counseling and psychotherapy of victims of organized violence. *Journal of Psychotherapy Integration, 11*, 241—262.

Reemtsma, J. (1997). Im Keller [In the cellar]. Hamburg, Germany: Hamburger Edition.

Straeter, B. (2003). Über Erfolg und Misserfolg von Kirchenasyl. [About success and failure of church asylum]. In W. D. Just & B. Straeter (Eds.), *Kirchenasyl. Ein Handbuch. [Church asylum. A handbook]* (pp. 164 —177). Karlsruhe, Germany: Von Loeper.

Yavuz, M.H. (1999). Search for a new social contract in Turkey: Fethullah Gulen, the Virtue Party and the Kurds. *SAIS Review of International Affairs, 19*(1), 114–143.